PAPIER MACHE
PROJECT BOOK

CONTENTS

Walter Foster

WHAT IS PAPIER-MACHE?

E very year, millions of tons of waste paper are thrown away—so we're going to show you a lot of fun and creative ways to recycle some of it.

Papier-mâché, which is French for "chewed paper," is an exciting way to make something out of waste paper. There are two main ways of making papier-mâché—pulping and layering.

For the pulping method, small pieces of paper are soaked in water until they disintegrate. Then they are mashed into a pulp, drained, squeezed almost dry, and then mixed with glue. The resulting pulp can be pressed into greased molds or used to add details to objects created with the layering method. If small amounts of pulp are needed, you can take a pasted strip of paper and scrunch it between your fingers to form a pellet of pulp.

Layering is the main method used in this book for making papier-mâché. This method involves layering strips of torn paper with glue and results in a very tough, but light, substance.

There are seven projects for you to try—but they are only a beginning. You'll have plenty of your own ideas once you start creating, and, as your confidence grows and you become more competent, you'll want to experiment with your new skills. You might even like to adapt the projects to reflect your own hobbies and interests.

It is a good idea to read the techniques section thoroughly before you embark on any projects so that you become familiar with the basic skills required and the materials you will need. Even if things seem a bit messy at first, it is worth persevering. You will find that it is great fun making your own creations from papier-mâché!

GETTING STARTED

What you need

Paper

First, and most obviously, you will need paper! All sorts of paper are suitable, and different papers will give different results. Collect a variety of papers – newspaper, computer printout paper, brown wrapping paper and even telephone directories – and test them for suitability. The lighter and thinner the paper you use, the smoother your finished objects will be.

For layering, where strips of paper are pasted on top of each other, it is best to use newspaper, as the layers bond together well and stick smoothly. Nearly everyone reads newspapers, so you shouldn't have any trouble collecting some! For pulping, where small pieces of paper are soaked in water, squeezed almost dry and mixed with glue, you can use almost any kind of paper, but do avoid all paper that is waxed or has a waterproof finish – this will look shiny – as it is not possible to break it down by soaking in water. As a general rule, the smoother and whiter the paper you use, the finer the pulp will be. Experiment with a variety of papers to discover which effects you like best.

Glue

So, having collected all your paper, you will need glue to stick it together. The best choice is cold-water wallpaper paste – be careful to use a brand that is nontoxic though. Wallpaper paste is easy to mix, and leftovers can be stored in an airtight container. If you spill some on your clothes, it won't stain, and it washes out easily. An alternative to wallpaper paste is sticky white craft glue. If you use it for making papier-mâché, you will need to dilute it first, by adding about twice as much water as glue. This glue dries more quickly than wallpaper paste and results in stronger papier-mâché, but it does have one big disadvantage: splashes won't wash out of clothes, carpets, or upholstery once they have dried, and you could become highly unpopular if you accidentally spill some! Again, if you do use white glue, remember to choose a nontoxic brand.

Apart from undiluted white glue, which is used in some projects to stick pieces of cardboard together, several projects also need nontoxic, strong, clear adhesive. Several brands of clear glue are suitable, but never use an epoxy-resin glue.

HELPFUL HINT . . .

If possible, use different colored paper for each layer of papier-mâché – it will enable you to see if you've completely covered the object with one layer before you begin the next and help to prevent uneven patches.

Equipment

Now that you have your main ingredients, you will also need some basic equipment. You will probably already have some **rulers** and **pencils**. Plastic rulers are fine for measuring pieces of cardboard, transferring measurements and so on, but when you have to cut straight lines, you should use a metal ruler. Your plastic ruler will eventually become chipped if you cut against it with a craft knife.

To mix the glue, whether you are using wallpaper paste or white glue, you will need a **large plastic bowl**. A kitchen sink is perfect, although it is a good idea to keep it to one side reserved especially for glue and to avoid using it for washing the dishes in, too.

A **craft knife** is very useful for cutting cardboard, especially if you are using the heavy-duty kind. However, you must be very, very careful with these knives, as their blades are extremely sharp. Always get an adult to help you at this stage in a project to prevent accidents.

You will need some **petroleum jelly** to grease molds before you put papier-mâché into them. The jelly creates a barrier between the mold and the paper, allowing the paper shape to be removed easily when it is dry – rather like a cake from a cake pan.

Modeling clay is very useful for making large, three-dimensional items such as puppet heads. You can make a sort of mold for the head by modeling it in clay first and then covering it with several layers of papier-mâché. Allow the paper to dry thoroughly, and then cut it open and remove the clay. Join the paper halves back together with strips of pasted paper. You can add facial features – ears and a nose, for example – to the head with small pellets of paper pulp.

A **palette-knife** with a thin blade is useful for helping to remove dry papier-mâché shapes from the sides of molds and for prying clay from the inside of finished pieces.

A **wire cake rack** is ideal for drying smaller items because it allows air to circulate freely around them. The pieces can be removed quite easily when they are dry.

Scissors are handy for cutting around shapes made from thin cardboard. Don't, however, use scissors to cut paper into strips – it should always be torn.

The finished projects are decorated with **poster paint**. There is a wide choice of colors available, but remember to check that you are using a nontoxic brand. The same applies to the **black India ink** that is used to outline designs – always use a nontoxic brand.

Masking tape is used in many of the projects to hold sections of cardboard together while they are drying. You can peel the tape from the card once the glue has set, but it will give extra strength to your constructions if you leave it in place and simply paper over it.

Cardboard is used to make the basic structure in several projects. Two different weights are used: **heavy corrugated cardboard** for larger items where strength is needed to avoid warping, and thinner card for such projects as the earrings. Empty boxes from the supermarket, electrical goods stores, and the like are ideal for heavy cardboard as long as they are clean and uncreased.

Clear gloss varnish was used to seal most of the projects in this book and to give them an attractive, shiny surface. Use a nontoxic brand. It is possible to buy a type of varnish that is made specifically for paper crafts such as papier-mâché, and this is quite safe. As with all the paints, glues, and inks used for these projects, an educational supplier or art store with a children's section will be able to tell you which brands are suitable. However, if you use a varnish that can only be cleaned off brushes with turpentine, ask an adult to help you, as turpentine can be dangerous if it is handled carelessly.

HELPFUL HINT . . .

Always use nontoxic glues and paints. Ask the store clerk for advice if you're in any doubt.

Techniques

Before you start any of the projects, read through all the instructions carefully to check how long the project will take you – many stages need to dry out overnight, so it is best to plan ahead.

Tearing paper

The length and width of your paper strips will vary according to what you are making. Pieces up to 3 in. (7.5cm) wide can be used if you are covering large, flat surfaces, but you will often find that you need much smaller pieces, some only as large as postage stamps.

When you are tearing up paper, bear in mind that it has a grain, like fabric, and it will tear much more easily in one direction than the other, usually – though not always – from the top to the bottom. Never cut paper into strips with scissors; this will give it a blunt, hard edge, which will show up when your object is painted and varnished.

Tear along the correct grain of the paper, as in the top picture. You can see, in the bottom picture, what happens if you do it the wrong way!

HELPFUL HINT . . .

Wash your hands when you have been tearing up newspaper. You will be surprised at how much ink comes off the paper!

Gluing

Your strips of paper should be covered on both sides with wallpaper paste or watered-down white glue. You can use your fingers or a brush to apply the glue, but don't use too much, or your object will take a long time to dry.

HELPFUL HINT . . .

Cover your worktop or table with old newspaper to prevent it from getting marked with splashes of glue or paint. Best of all, use a plastic sheet, which can be wiped clean when you have finished work for the day.

Using a mold

All sorts of objects can be used as molds for papier-mâché. Bowls, plates, and dishes are ideal. Always smear petroleum jelly over the mold before you use it, or it will be very difficult to remove the dried paper shape. Cardboard is also a good "mold" or base – but it will be left inside the paper as a permanent part of the structure. Several layers can be built up on top of cardboard to make a good, strong base.

Drying

The time each piece will take to dry will depend on its size and the number of layers of papier-mâché you have used. Usually, 24 hours is adequate for a cardboard shape with two or three layers of paper on it, but a balloon with eight layers of papier-mâché may take up to 3 days to dry. Use a warm place to dry your papier-mâché.

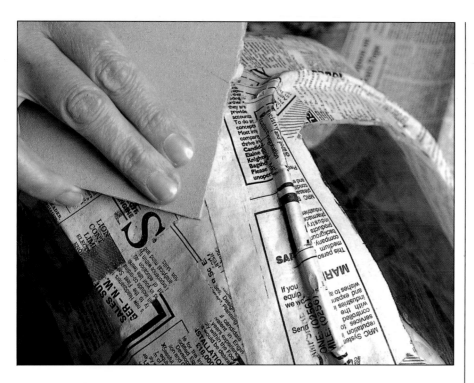

HELPFUL HINT . . .

Wear a plastic apron or a pair of overalls when you make papier-mâché – it can be quite messy.

Sanding

When your papier-mâché is dry, you should lightly rub down the surface with fine sandpaper. This will remove any wrinkles in the paper and give you a smoother surface to paint on.

Priming

Use two coats of white paint to prime the surface of your papier-mâché. This will cover up newsprint effectively, gives a bright ground to paint on, and will make your colors seem more luminous. You must let the first coat dry before adding the second, or the paint may crack. If this happens, let the paint dry, sand it back to the paper, and start again. Always use nontoxic paint.

Decorating

When you have primed the papier-mâché, it can be decorated with poster paint. You will have to thin the paint with water, and you will probably need to use two coats to achieve a good, deep color. Black India ink, which is waterproof, can be used to accentuate the painted designs. Apply it with a thin paint-brush and use a nontoxic brand.

Earrings

These bright flower earrings look very attractive. Although they are quite large, they are very light, and you could make them even larger or longer without weighing your ears down.

Other motifs that would look good include hearts, stars, and fish. You could make several pairs when you have learned the basic technique. The earrings are attached to the ears by clips, which are stuck to the backs of the yellow disks with strong glue.

EARRINGS TEMPLATES *(Thin cardboard)*

Making the earrings

1 Trace the earring shapes from the pattern above and transfer them to the thin cardboard.

2 Cut around the shapes with a craft knife or scissors. **Ask an adult to help you if you use a craft knife, because it will have a very sharp blade.** Paint your cutout shapes with one coat of watered-down white glue. Lay them on a wire cake rack for 4 hours to dry.

YOU WILL NEED

Tracing paper • Thin cardboard approximately 4 x 4 in. (10 x 10cm) • Craft knife or scissors • Wallpaper paste or watered-down white glue • Paper • Fine sandpaper • Poster paints • Black India ink • Clear gloss varnish • Darning needle • White glue (undiluted) • 2 pairs of earring hooks and eyes • Strong, clear glue • 1 pair of clip fastenings • Small pair of pliers

---

HELPFUL HINT . . .

Knives, especially craft knives, can be dangerous. Always hold what you are cutting very carefully, and cut away from you. Better still, ask an adult to help you.

3 Using small strips of paper, about ½ in. × 2 in. (12mm × 5cm), cover the earring shapes with three layers of pasted paper. Work carefully around each petal, making sure that your papier-mâché does not become too lumpy so that it will have a smooth finish. Lay the papered shapes on a cake rack to dry for 24 hours.

4 When the shapes are completely dry, smooth them down lightly with fine sandpaper and coat them with two layers of white paint, allowing the first to dry before you add the second. Draw the center of the daisy on your flower shapes. The petal outlines and swirls will be drawn freehand on top of the poster paint later with black India ink.

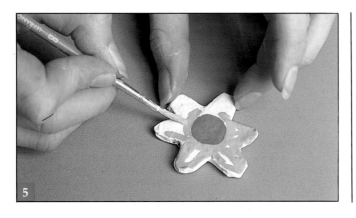

5 Start to fill in the color. The petals were painted light blue, and then, when this coat was dry, they were painted again in violet, with the light blue allowed to show through in patches. The disks have been given two coats of yellow paint.

When you have painted all the pieces, allow them to dry for 4 hours.

6 Then, using a fine paintbrush, carefully draw in the black outlines and swirls. Let the earrings dry

overnight, then varnish the fronts with clear gloss varnish. Lay the pieces (varnished side up!) on a wire cake rack to dry. Varnish the backs and allow them to dry again. Repeat the process so that the fronts and backs have two coats of varnish.

7 When the second coat of varnish is dry, make a small hole with a darning needle in the top of the petal section and in the bottom of the disk. Dab a little undiluted white glue into the holes. Push an earring hook section into the hole in each flower and an eye into each disk.

8 Dab some strong, clear glue onto the earring clips, and position one on the back of each disk. Press the disk and clip together firmly, and let all the earring pieces dry overnight.

9 Loop the hook into the eye, joining the disk and the flower, and close the opening with a small pair of pliers. Your earrings are now ready to wear!

Barnacle Bowl

*In addition to using some of the basic techniques involved in making papier-mâché, this bowl is made from **two** separate pieces which have to be joined together. The main part of the bowl is made by laying thin strips of paper in a greased mold, while a smaller mold is used to make the "foot" that the bowl stands on. The bowl and foot are joined together with strips of papier-mâché, and their edges are bound with cord and covered to create a rim.*

YOU WILL NEED

Two plastic bowls, one about 8 in. (20cm) in diameter, one about 3 in. (7.5cm) in diameter • Petroleum jelly • Paper • Wallpaper paste or watered-down white glue • Blunt knife or palette-knife • Scissors • Preshrunk piping cord • Masking tape • White glue (undiluted) • Fine sandpaper • Poster paints • Black India ink • Clear gloss varnish

The body of the bowl illustrated is made in a plastic bowl with a diameter of about 8 in. (20cm), and the foot is made from a straight-sided margarine tub. Whatever bowls you choose, make sure that they look balanced together and as if they are meant to be joined.

The bowl is decorated with little pellets of paper pulp, which are applied in a regular pattern and painted in bright colors. Paper pulp is a very effective method of adding decoration to papier-mâché items, and quite ornate designs can be built up very quickly so that even rather plain shapes can be transformed into exciting articles.

The bowl can be used to hold a variety of dry objects, especially fruit, although you may want to choose varieties that don't clash with your color scheme! Don't keep wet things in it, however – it won't be waterproof, and you may spoil the varnished surface.

Making the bowl

1 Grease the insides of the molds with a little petroleum jelly so that the papier-mâché shapes can be easily removed when they are dry. Tear your paper into strips 1–1½ in. (2.5–4cm) wide and long enough to fit the bowl from one side to the other with about 1 in. (2.5cm) of excess paper on each edge. Begin to lay your pasted paper in the bowl, making sure that the strips lie flat against the walls. Continue to lay the paper in the bowl, covering the edge of the strip you have just put in place with the next strip. You may have to fan the strips out slightly as you move around the bowl so that the papier-mâché does not crease.

2 When you have finished the first layer of paper, start the second, laying the strips at right angles to the first layer, to give a good, strong bowl. Add eight layers of strips. Leave the papier-mâché to dry in a warm place for 48 hours.

3 When the surface of the bowl feels dry, gently insert the blade of a blunt knife or a palette-knife between the paper and mold, and ease the paper shells away from the sides. Lay the shape upside-down in a warm place to dry for a few hours.

4 The edges of your paper shapes will need sealing to stop them from coming apart. Use scissors to trim the excess paper back to within ¼ in. (5mm) of the edge of your bowl.

5 Then take a pasted strip of paper, about 1 in. (2.5cm) wide, and fully overlap the cut edge, tearing off the excess strip as you reach the back of the bowl each time. One layer of binding strips will be enough.

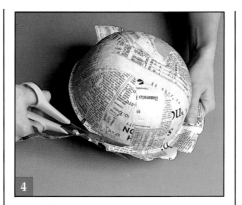

6 Leave the bound edges to dry and then place the piping cord around the outside edges of the bowl, pushing the cord right up against the lip of the rim. Secure the ends of the cord together with masking tape and tape the cord in place at several points around the rim. Then cover the cord with strips of paper, exactly as you did when you sealed the cut edges. Cover the cord with three layers of papier-mâché, and let the bowl dry for 24 hours.

Making the foot

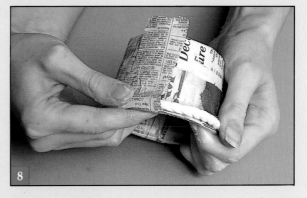

7 Grease the inside of the foot and lay in the strips of paper as you did in the bowl. Lay each of the 8 layers in at different angles to one another, and leave to dry out for 48 hours, before easing the paper cast out of the mold.

8 Trim back the paper as in step 4 and bind the edges with small pieces of paper. Leave to dry and then wrap the cord around the rim as in step 6. Secure it and seal with 3 layers of papier-mâché and allow it to dry for 24 hours.

Joining the foot to the bowl

9 Now dab some undiluted white glue on the top of the foot section and position it squarely under the body. Tape the two together with masking tape and leave the glue to dry for a couple of hours. Place a piece of cord around the join (a), tape it in place, and cover it with three layers of papier-mâché (b). Leave the bowl to dry for 24 hours.

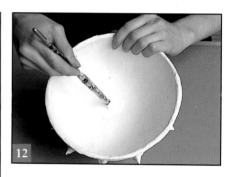

10 When your bowl is completely dry, you can make it more ornate with paper pulp additions if you wish. To make the "barnacles," take a strip of paper about 1 in. (2.5cm) wide and 8 in. (20cm) long. Coat it with glue and squash it into a pellet.

11 Then simply press the pellet firmly to the outside of your bowl to fix it, repeating the process as many times as you wish. If you want the "barnacles" to have a smooth surface, cover them with very short, thin strips of paper, say ¼ in. (5mm) wide and 1½ in. (4cm) long. Leave your bowl to dry for 24 hours.

12 When it is dry, smooth the bowl with fine sandpaper and paint it with two coats of white poster paint, allowing the first coat to dry thoroughly before adding the next.

13 Paint the rope bands in colors that contrast with the body – you will probably need two coats of color to cover the white paint completely – then paint the "barnacles" in whatever colors appeal to you.

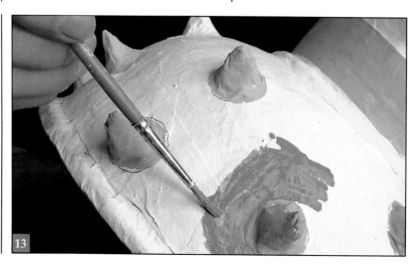

14 Let the paint dry for 3–4 hours and paint contrasting black ink lines on your bowl using a fine paint-brush. Leave the bowl to dry for 24 hours.

15 Give your bowl two coats of clear gloss varnish, allowing the first coat to dry thoroughly before adding the second. Remember to clean your varnishing brush with soap and water when you have finished.

Decorative Eggs

These decorative eggs are made using modeling clay as a mold. A piece of thin cardboard is used to make a lip to hold the two halves together.

If you are giving the eggs as decorative gifts, you might like to put little presents – charms or candy, for example – inside them as a surprise.

Making the Decorative Eggs

1 Break the clay into lumps that are about the size you want each finished egg to be. Roll each piece of clay between the palms of your hands to soften it, and then work it into an egg shape. Add or take away clay as necessary, and finally cover the eggs with petroleum jelly.

2 When you are satisfied with your egg shapes, tear up your paper into pieces about the size of postage stamps and start to cover the eggs. Try to mold the paper smoothly over the clay. Cover each egg shape with eight layers of papier-mâché, and leave them to dry in a warm place for 2–3 days.

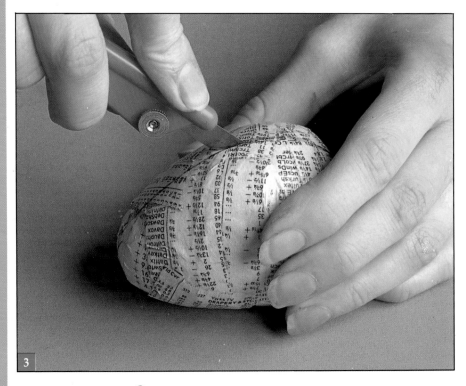

3 When the papier-mâché feels dry, ask an adult to cut each egg into two equal halves. It is probably easiest to make the first cut with a craft knife through the papier-mâché to the clay all the way around each egg, and then to use a kitchen knife with a serrated blade – a bread knife, for example – to saw through the clay.

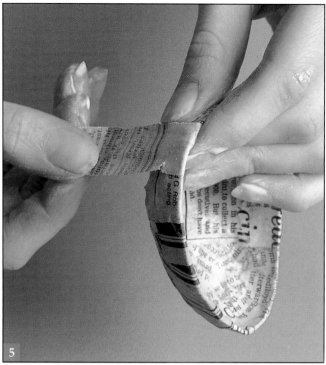

5 Bind all around the cut edges of each empty shell with small strips of paper, approximately ½ × 2 in. (12mm × 5cm). One layer of binding strips will be sufficient. Let the shells dry overnight on a wire cake rack.

4 Leave the opened eggs to dry on a wire cake rack for an hour or so, and then, using the blade of a thin palette-knife, gently prize the clay away from the walls of each papier-mâché egg.

6 Lightly sand the shells inside and out, and give each one two coats of white poster paint, allowing the first coat to dry thoroughly before you add the second.

7 Draw designs on the outside of the painted shells and start to fill them in with color. You will probably need two coats of paint to achieve a good, deep color.

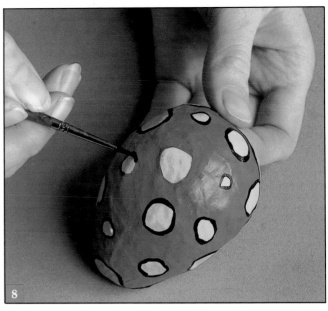

8 Allow the paint to dry for 4 hours, and outline your designs with black India ink. Let the eggs dry overnight.

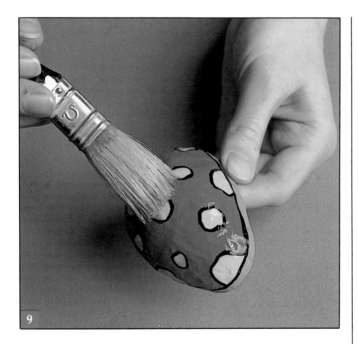

9 Give each eggshell two coats of clear gloss varnish. Paint the varnish on one side at a time, and let it dry completely before you do the other. Allow the first coat to dry on each side of your eggs before you add the second.

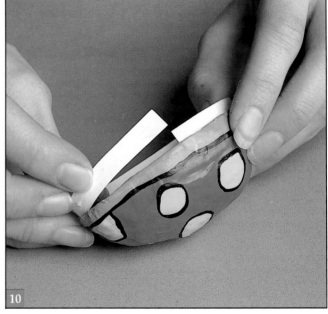

10 Measure around the inside edge of one half of each egg. Cut a piece of thin white cardboard this length and about ½ in. (12mm) wide. Coat the card with clear, strong glue down one long edge, and spread a thin line of the same glue around the inside edge of one eggshell. Let the glue on both surfaces dry slightly and press the card around the inside of the eggshell. Make sure the ends join neatly.

11 Let your eggs dry thoroughly before you fit them together.

Jointed Elephant

This handsome elephant has movable legs, ears, and tail. His body is made from thick cardboard, while thinner cardboard is used for his limbs, ears, and tail, which are held in place with paper brads. These brads, which can be bought from stationery shops, act as pivots and allow you to reposition the elephant's limbs.

YOU WILL NEED

Tracing paper ● Thick cardboard ● Thin cardboard ● Scissors ● Craft knife ● Wallpaper paste or watered-down white glue ● Paper ● Fine sandpaper ● 7 paper brads ● Masking tape ● Poster paints ● Black India ink ● Clear gloss varnish.

JOINTED ELEPHANT TEMPLATES *(Thick and thin cardboard)*

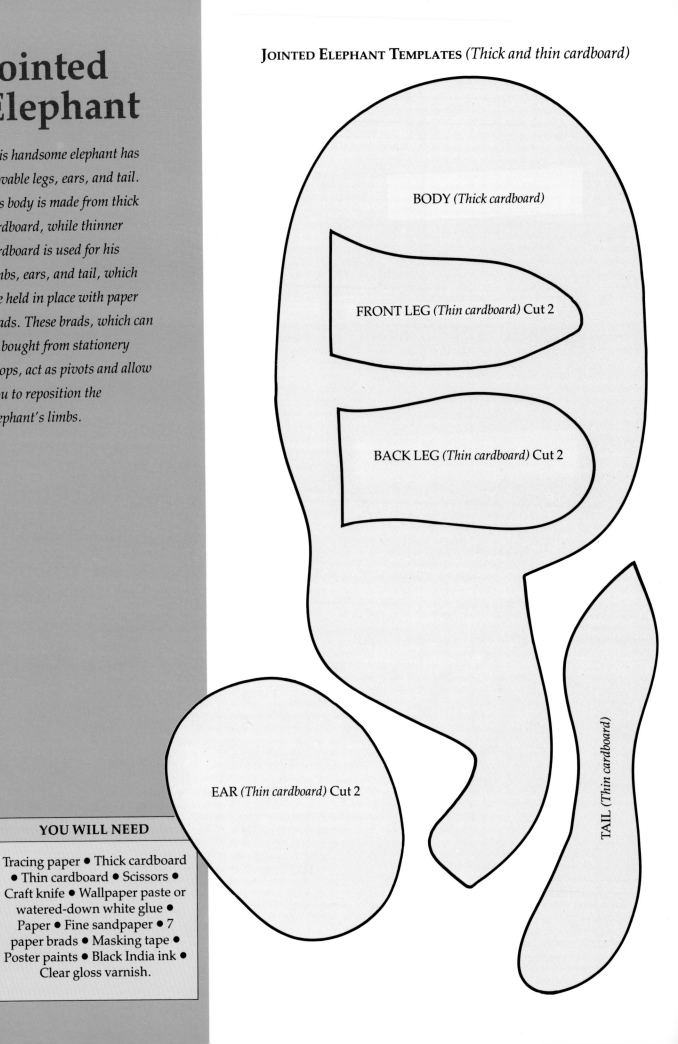

BODY *(Thick cardboard)*

FRONT LEG *(Thin cardboard)* Cut 2

BACK LEG *(Thin cardboard)* Cut 2

EAR *(Thin cardboard)* Cut 2

TAIL *(Thin cardboard)*

Making your elephant

1 Trace the elephant pieces from the pattern and transfer them to the cardboard. Remember to use thick cardboard for the body and thinner card for the movable parts. Cut around each piece with scissors. Ask an adult to help you cut the thicker cardboard, as the craft knife will be very sharp.

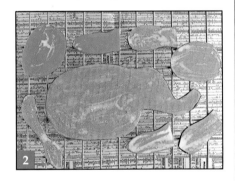

2 When all the pieces are cut, give them a coat of watered-down white glue to help prevent them from warping when papier-mâché is added. Leave the pieces to dry on a wire cake rack for 4 hours.

3 Tear your paper into thin, short strips, ½ in. (12mm) wide and 3 in. (7.5cm) long, and cover the pieces of cardboard with three coats of papier-mâché. Leave the shapes to dry overnight on a wire cake rack.

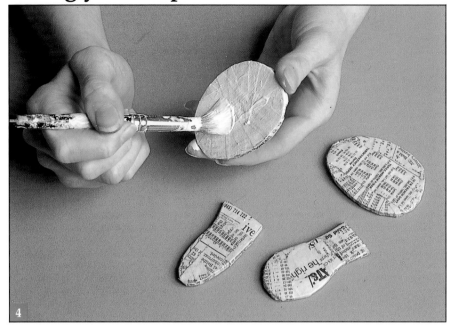

4 When the shapes are dry, smooth them with fine sandpaper and give each one two coats of white poster paint, taking care to let the paint dry thoroughly between each coat.

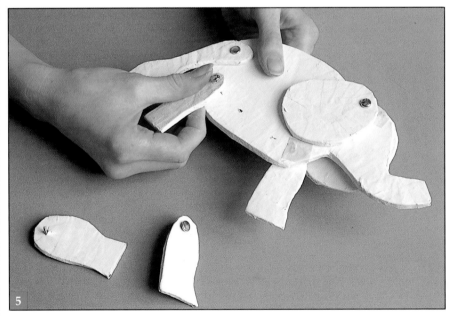

5 The legs, ears, and tail are joined to the body with brads. So that the shanks of each brad can pass through the cardboard, you have to make a small incision toward the top center of each movable piece. Ask an adult to help you with this, because you need a craft knife, which will have a very sharp blade. Pass the shanks of a brad through each little hole. Ask an adult to help you make similar incisions in the elephant's body for the brads to pass through. You need to make seven holes, one for each of the legs and ears and one for the tail. Remember that some pins have to go from the front to the back of the body and some from the back to the front, but you can make room for them by moving each piece to one side once it has been fixed.

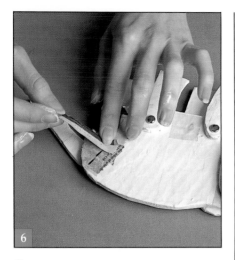

6 When all the brads are in place, cover the opened-out shanks of each one with masking tape. Cover the tape with strips of papier-mâché, and leave your elephant to dry overnight, propped upright if possible.

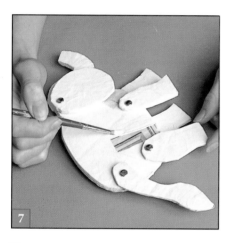

7 When the papier-mâché is dry, carefully sand it down and give the elephant two coats of white paint, allowing the first to dry completely before you add the second.

HELPFUL HINT . . .
Leave your papier-mâché objects in the driest place in the house – but away from direct heat.

Painting your elephant

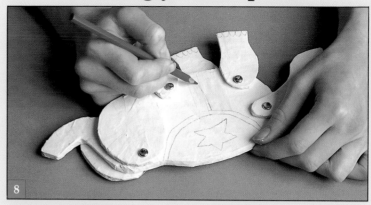

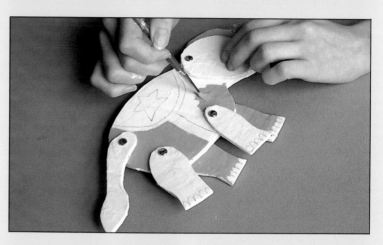

8 Draw in the elephant's toenails, tusks, eye, and blanket, and paint the elephant with poster paints. You will have to move his limbs carefully so that you can paint him properly, and you will probably have to come back to the underside of his ears and legs several times because you won't be able to paint everything all at once. Remember that your elephant has two sides, so paint both sides the same.

9 When you have finished painting the colors in, let your elephant dry for 4 hours, and then add the outlines and details in black India ink. Leave your elephant to dry overnight, and then give him two coats of clear gloss varnish, allowing the first coat to dry thoroughly before you add the second. When you are varnishing around his limbs, take care that they don't stick to his body. When you have finished varnishing, clean your brush thoroughly with soap and water.

Hinged Box

This box, which closes with a hinged lid, is decorated with a technique known as découpage. *This involves collecting interesting scraps from such sources as magazines, newspapers, and greeting cards. The cutout scraps are stuck onto objects as a decoration and varnished in place.*

This box has been decorated with black and white engravings that were photocopied from an old encyclopedia, but almost anything that you like would be suitable.

YOU WILL NEED

Thick cardboard, approximately 16 × 14 in. (40 × 36cm) ● Craft knife ● White glue (undiluted) ● Masking tape ● Wallpaper paste or watered-down white glue ● Paper ● Fine sandpaper ● Cotton ribbon, 1 in. (2.5cm) wide and 4 in. (10cm) long ● An assortment of scraps cut from newspapers, magazines, greeting cards, wallpaper books, etc. ● Clear gloss varnish

HINGED BOX TEMPLATE *(Thick cardboard)*

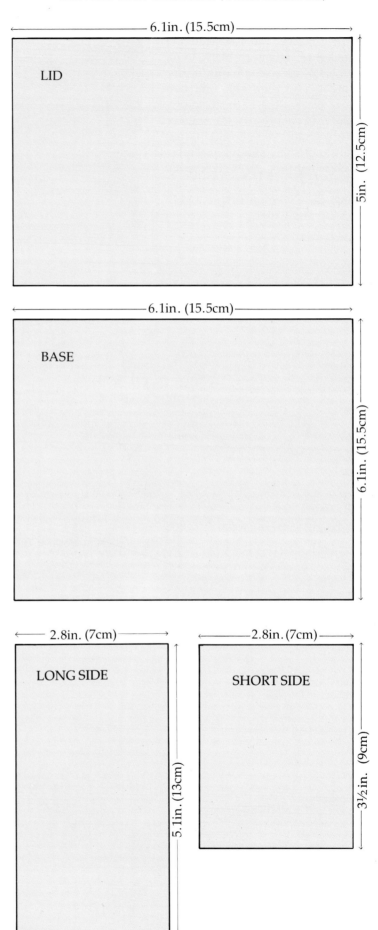

Making the hinged box

1 Accurately transfer the measurements for each piece of the box from the diagram in the book onto the cardboard. Ask an adult to cut each piece out for you with a craft knife and metal ruler. Take the pieces of cardboard that make up the sides and smear the edges with white glue. Join them at right angles and secure the joins firmly with masking tape.

2 Give all the pieces of the box a coat of watered-down white glue and leave them to dry for 4 hours on a wire cake rack. Cover the underside of the joined side section with white glue, and place it squarely on the base. Tape the joins together with masking tape. Leave the glue to set for an hour or so, and then cover the box pieces with three layers of papier-mâché. Let them dry overnight on a wire cake rack.

3 When the papier-mâché is dry, smooth it down with fine sandpaper. Fold the piece of ribbon in two along its length and coat half its width with undiluted glue. Press the glued ribbon along the back top edge of the box body. Put glue on the other half of the ribbon, and press it onto the box lid. You will probably have to support the lid on a pile of magazines or one or two books while the glue dries. Cover the edges of the ribbon hinge with two layers of papier-mâché, avoiding the crease along the center, and let it rest on its support for 24 hours.

4 When it is completely dry, lightly sand the extra papier-mâché around the hinge and give the whole box two coats of white poster paint.

5 Let the paint dry thoroughly, and then start to arrange your cutout scraps, trying out several designs before you glue them down. Use a little undiluted glue to stick the scraps to the box, and leave them to dry for a few hours in a warm place.

6 If you are leaving some of the box surface white, use watered-down glue, but not too much, as a varnish, since clear gloss varnish tends to look slightly yellow on top of white. Otherwise, use clear gloss varnish. Whichever you use, give your box two coats, allowing the first coat to dry thoroughly before you apply the second. Leave your box to dry for 24 hours before you use it.

Square Frame with Heart-shaped Opening

This frame has a distinctive heart-shaped opening. It has a hinge and is fastened at one side with a thin ribbon bow.

Although this design would be good to give as a Valentine's Day present, you could make the opening any shape you like and make the frame as large or as small as you please. You could even have several openings in the frame and keep a variety of pictures or photographs in it.

YOU WILL NEED

Thick cardboard, approximately 14 × 14 in. (36 × 36cm) ● Craft knife ● White glue ● Masking tape ● Wallpaper paste or watered down white glue ● Paper ● Fine sandpaper ● Cotton tape, 1 in. (2.5cm) wide and 8 in. (20cm) long ● Narrow cotton ribbon, 8 in. (20cm) long ● Strong, clear glue ● Poster paints ● Black India ink ● Clear gloss varnish ● Black felt, approximately 7 × 7 in. (17.5 × 17.5cm) ● Scissors

SQUARE FRAME WITH HEART-SHAPED OPENING TEMPLATE *(Thick cardboard)*

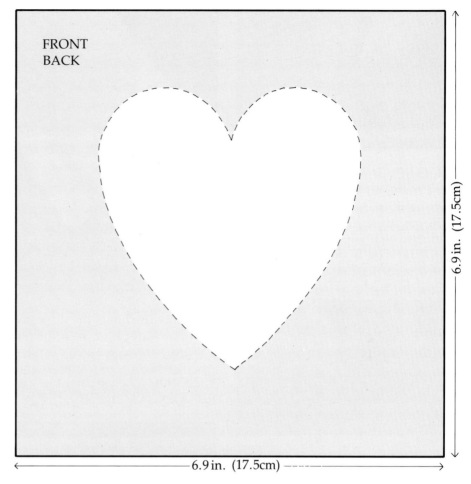

FRONT
BACK

6.9 in. (17.5cm)

6.9 in. (17.5cm)

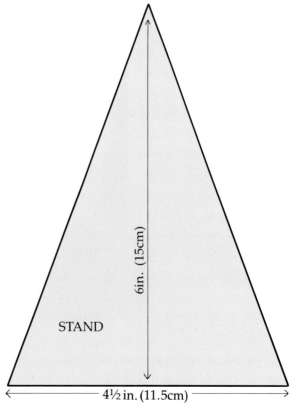

STAND

6in. (15cm)

4½ in. (11.5cm)

Making your frame

1 Mark out the measurements for the front and back of the frame on the cardboard. Be sure to transfer the measurements correctly. Ask an adult to help you cut out the frame and stand pieces with a craft knife, because the knife will be very sharp.

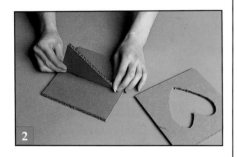

2 Measure a point halfway along the top and bottom edges of the back. Use a ruler to join these two points with a pencil line. Coat one long edge of the stand with white glue and place it along the line on the back. Hold the stand firmly in position with masking tape and leave the glue to set for a couple of hours.

3 Give the frame pieces a coat of watered-down white glue, and let them dry on a wire cake rack for 4 hours. Cover all the pieces with three layers of papier-mâché. Make sure that you do not knock the stand out of position. Let the frame pieces dry on a wire cake rack overnight.

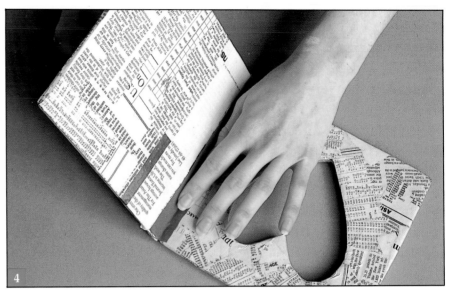

4 Lightly rub down the dry pieces with fine sandpaper. Fold the tape you are going to use as the hinge in two lengthwise and spread undiluted white glue on half of it. Glue the tape to the right-hand edge of the inside of the front of the frame. Smear glue on the other half of the tape, and stick it to the edge of the back. While the tape is drying, prop the frame slightly open so that it doesn't stick to itself.

5 When the tape is dry, open the frame. Measure two points, one halfway down the inside of the left-hand side of the front of the frame and one halfway down the right-hand side of the back. Mark these points and glue half the length of narrow ribbon to each with strong clear glue. Hold the lengths of ribbon in place with masking tape. Cover the edges of the hinge tape and the ribbon with two layers of papier-mâché. Leave the frame to dry for 24 hours.

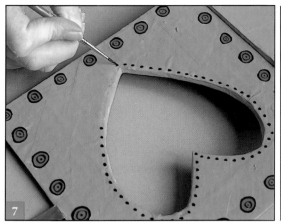

6 Lightly sand the extra papier-mâché, and give your frame two coats of white poster paint, allowing the first coat to dry before you add the second. Leave to dry.

7 Draw a design on the frame with pencil and fill it in with color. Don't forget to paint the back, too. Allow the paint to dry for 4 hours and then add detail to your design with black Indian ink. Let the frame dry overnight and then apply two coats of clear gloss varnish.

8 Take the piece of black felt and use scissors to cut it to the same size as the back. Smear it with undiluted fabric glue, and stick it carefully to the back so that it covers the edge of the thin ribbon. Let your frame dry overnight before you use it.

Monster Mask

This monster mask is made over a balloon mold, but the resulting paper shape is cut around rather than lengthwise, so that it fits over the head like a helmet. The monster has strange, golden protruberances growing from the top of its head and seven eyes, but the effect is humorous rather than scary.

The golden spikes have been made with empty cones from rolls of yarn, but if you can't find these, you can make your own cones from rolled-up cardboard just as easily.

YOU WILL NEED

Tape measure • 1 balloon • Petroleum jelly • Paper • Wallpaper paste or watered-down white glue • String • Scissors • Craft knife • White glue (undiluted) • 6 empty knitting wool cones or cones made of thin cardboard • Masking tape • Fine sandpaper • Poster paints • Black India ink • Nontoxic gold craft paint • Clear gloss varnish

Making a monster mask

1 Measure around your head, holding the tape measure over the mid-point of your ears. Blow up the balloon – you may need an adult to help you at this point – until it is slightly larger at its widest point than your head measurement. Tie the balloon tightly, and grease it with a thin coat of petroleum jelly. Stand the balloon in an empty bowl.

2 Tear the paper into strips about 1 in. (2.5cm) wide and 10 in. (25cm) long and cover the balloon with eight layers of papier-mâché. If possible, use two colors of paper alternately so that you can see when you have finished each layer. Tie a length of string to the end, and hang your balloon to dry in a warm place for 2–3 days.

3 When the papier-mâché is dry, burst the balloon by sticking a pin through it; pull the deflated balloon through the bottom of the cast. Measure a line from the center of the top of your head down the front of your face to the bridge of your nose. This line should be long enough to reach to about 1 in. (2.5cm) below your eyes. Transfer this measurement to the front of your balloon. Make a pencil mark at the center of the balloon, measure straight down until you have the same length as the distance from the top of your head to your nose and make a mark. Repeat this measurement from the same central point several times, working your way around the balloon until you have a row of dots. Join this line of dots and ask an adult to help you cut along it with sharp scissors.

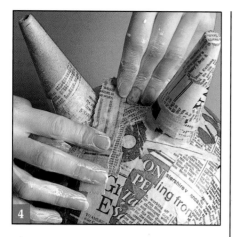

4 Place the paper "helmet" over your head, and hold the paper between finger and thumb, fingers outside and thumbs directly in front of each eye – your fingers will show you where. Ask someone to help you mark the spots on the outside of the mask. Draw in two eye shapes, and ask an adult to help you cut out these shapes with a craft knife. **Never** try to make the eye holes while you are wearing the mask. Arrange the cones, about 4 in. (10cm) high, on the crown of your mask. When you are happy with their position, draw around the base of each. Coat the underside of each cone with white glue, and place them back in position inside the drawn lines. Hold them firmly in position with masking tape. Let the glue set for a couple of hours, then cover the cones with two layers of papier-mâché. Make sure that you cover the joins well.

5 Bind around the cutout eyes and around the edge of the mask with small pieces of papier-mâché. Stand it on a wire cake rack to dry for 24 hours. When the mask is dry, sand it lightly with fine sandpaper and give it two coats of white paint, allowing the first coat to dry thoroughly before you add the second.

Painting the mask

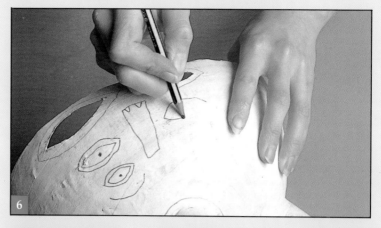

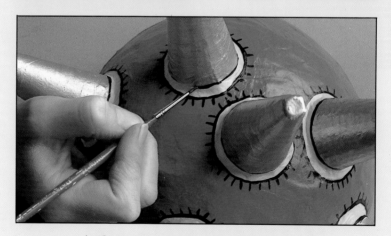

6 When the paint has dried, draw a design on the mask and start to fill it in with color. The mask illustrated here has been decorated very simply, but it would lend itself perfectly to more flamboyant designs. When you have finished painting your mask, let it dry for 4 hours and then outline your design with black India ink. Paint the spikes with gold craft paint, and leave the mask to dry for 24 hours.

7 The mask should now be painted with two coats of clear gloss varnish, but be careful not to varnish over the gold paint on the spikes. Let the first coat of varnish dry before adding the second coat, and remember to clean your brushes in warm soapy water when you have finished.

Self-Portrait With Seven Fingers, *1912/13 - Oil on canvas, 126 x 107 cm - Amsterdam, Stedelijk Museum*

CHAGALL

"Her silences are my silences, her eyes are my eyes. It is as if Bella had known me forever, as if she knew all my childhood, all my present and all my future... She is my eyes, indeed my soul!"

Marc Chagall, *Ma Vie, 1931*

Marc Chagall, among the most original and poetic of 20th century painters, does not belong to any one school of art nor to any of the numerous movements which hailed his genius. The intellectual approach to art of many of his contemporaries never appealed to him. Instead, throughout his long life, he returned constantly to the magical memories of his Russian childhood to create some of the most colourful and popular art of the century.

Marc Chagall was born in the Byelorussian (western Russian) town of Vitebsk on 7 July 1887. Chagall's father was a fishmonger's assistant, a serious man and a devout Hasidic Jew who survived in Chagall's memory as a weary figure in a prayer shawl, reciting prayers. This weariness is understandable; Chagall was one of nine children - he had seven sisters and a brother. His mother, an indomitably energetic woman, ran a small haberdasher's shop and the Chagall household hummed with visiting relatives, friends and customers. All were Jewish, as was half the population of Vitebsk.

The Chagall house was one of many simple wooden dwellings

Chagall working in his studio in Vence

with small vegetable gardens running down to the banks of the River Dvina. In and around their courtyards chickens strutted and goats and white cows wandered. The young Chagall saw these animals as companions to talk to; later, they would appear repeatedly in his art.

So, too, would the roofs and towers of the churches, monasteries and synagogues of Vitebsk, which Chagall could see rising on the hills beyond his home. Seen from the dormer window of his childhood bedroom, these domes and spires assumed a fantastical, legendary quality. Closer to home, the streets below his window were thronged with the domestic dramas and comedies of local Jewish life.

To be a Jew in Czarist Russia was, however, a serious disadvantage. Anti-semitism was rife and officially sanctioned; Chagall's mother had to resort to bribery to get him into the local school, in theory barred to Jews. His mother had hoped Chagall would become a clerk; but a schoolfriend, seeing some of Chagall's first drawings, called him an artist. The word was unknown in the Chagall household but now Chagall decided that he would become an artist, despite his father's appalled protests.

In Vitebsk Chagall took his first art lessons from a local painter called Jeshua Pen, but Saint Petersburg (now Leningrad) beckoned and in the spring of 1907 he enrolled in a semi-public art school in the capital. There he also encountered anti-semitism; Jews were banned officially from the city unless they had business there, and at one point Chagall had to pretend to be a lawyer's footman to deceive the police. At first Chagall found neither the official art course nor urban life inspiring. Then, in the autumn of 1908, Leon Bakst (1886-1925), a painter and stage designer who was also Jewish, returned to Saint Petersburg from Paris; Chagall joined his new Zvantseva art school.

Bakst offered openings to a far wider world than Chagall had hitherto encountered. At his studio he learnt of Post-Impressionism, Symbolism and Fauvism. For Chagall their brilliant colours were an intoxication and revelation.

In *My Fiancée With Black Gloves* (page 4), a striking work from these student days, Chagall created a completely novel image. His fiancée was Bella Rosenfeld, daughter of a Jewish bourgeois family whom he had met in 1909 whilst on holiday in Vitebsk. Bella

became his muse and idol but they could not then marry as Chagall was almost penniless.

Instead, Chagall went to Paris. Bakst had announced he was joining the Ballet Russe in Paris, the company founded by the impresario Diaghilev, which created modern ballet. Chagall managed to persuade a lawyer, who had bought two of his works, to pay for his ticket and provide a tiny allowance. Armed with this, he set out for Paris in the late summer of 1910.

He hailed Paris as a "city of light and liberty". Although at first unable to speak a word of French, he wandered the streets in a delighted haze, free from the tyranny of Czarist Russia. In 1912 he moved to the artists' colony of La Ruche, in a poor quarter of Paris near slaughterhouses, home to many immigrant artists. He visited the Louvre frequently, where he admired the great masters -Veronese, Rembrandt and Delacroix - but it was contemporary works which inspired him most, especially the Fauvists and Cubists. The former he admired for their uninhibited use of colour, the latter for their fragmenting of form. But he felt that both were over-intellectual in their approach compared to his own, very intuitive, art, and the

Drawing from My Life, 1922/23

Cubists' moves towards complete abstraction especially repelled him.

It was in the four years after his arrival in Paris that Chagall created his own, totally original art. At first the influence of the Post-Impressionists, especially Van Gogh, was strongest, as in the searing colours of *The Sabbath* (page 6), but Chagall's roots lay in a more magical but less intense art than the Dutchman's. Above all, he was already looking back to Russia.

This is very obvious in his *Self-Portrait With Seven Fingers* (page 1). Both Cubist and Fauvist influences are evident in its form but in content this painting could only be by Chagall. The seven fingers refers presumably to the seven-branched candlestick of Judaism; other symbols are less esoteric. Behind the painter looms Paris, but he has his back to it and is busy painting a brilliant vermilion cow all the time thinking, in the bubble of thought since popularised by strip-cartoonists, of Russia. Most of his other paintings of these early, crucial years also reveal a visionary nostalgia for his birthplace, such as *I And The Village* (page 8) or *To Russia, Asses And Others* (page 10).

This was an art too original and spontaneous for Chagall's fellow painters, locked in their intellectual disputes, to appreciate fully. The poets Guillaume Apollinaire and Blaise Cendrars, however, recognised his genius. They introduced him to the German art dealer Herwarth Walden, who invited him to exhibit at Der Sturm Gallery in Berlin. Chagall accepted and in May 1914 set off with his many canvases to Berlin. The exhibition made his name in Germany, where his "magical realism" paralleled that of the radical Blaue Reiter School (a group of avant-garde painters headed by Kandinsky). Chagall decided to visit Vitebsk for a holiday in July. There, the outbreak of the First World War entrapped him.

He was, however, finally able to marry Bella Rosenfeld in 1915 and they had a daughter in

Self-portrait In Front Of The Easel, 1922/23 - Etching from Ma Vie.

1916. Despite public disasters, they were ecstatically happy together - a happiness he celebrated again and again in paintings from *The Birthday* of 1915 (page 14) to *To My Wife* of 1944 (page 24). In 1918 the new Communist government made Chagall Commissar of Art for Vitebsk. Chagall was not unsympathetic to the new regime but he was utterly unsuited to run art schools in such chaotic times. When the abstract painter Malevich arrived and began attacking his art, Chagall fled - first to Moscow, where he nearly starved to death but did some work for the Jewish Theatre, and then finally back to Paris in 1923. He never returned to Russia.

In France the dealer Ambroise Vollard commissioned him to illustrate many books, including Gogol's *Dead Souls* and La Fontaine's *Fables*. Soon Chagall became internationally popular and he was able to travel extensively - to Italy, Spain, the Near East and Holland. The *Equestrienne* series (page 22) painted around this time shows the classical elegance of his style. The Surrealists hailed him as a fellow artist for his dream-like images such as *Time Is A River Without Banks* (page 24) but he always remained

aloof from any one artistic school.

He could not, however, ignore the worsening international situation as Europe slid towards the Second World War. Paintings such as *The White Crucifixion* (page 26) reflect his concern with the Nazi persecutions of the Jews. When France fell in 1940, he managed to escape with Bella to New York. There he worked on commissions for ballet and theatre designs besides painting more private pictures, again often on the theme of the crucifixion with a Jewish slant.

In 1944, quite suddenly, Bella died. Chagall was heartbroken and sank for a time into a torpor, only reviving when Stravinsky commissioned him to paint the scenery for his ballet *The Firebird.*

After the Second World War Chagall returned to France, settling finally in Saint-Paul-de-Vence in Provence. In 1952 he married Valentine Brodsky. His last years seemed to offer the stability and repose he had lacked too often. International commissions and honours poured in, from decorating the University Clinic Synagogue in Jerusalem to painting the ceiling for the Paris Opéra. His style became ever freer and more dream-like in his last years. He died in 1985.

Lovers By The Palisade, 1922/23 - Etching from Ma Vie

MY FIANCEE WITH BLACK GLOVES

1909 - Oil on canvas, 88 x 65 cm
Basle, Kunstmuseum

Chagall with Bella in a photograph from 1910, shortly before his departure for Paris.

Bella With Carnation, 1925 - Oil on canvas, 100 x 80 cm - Basle, Meyer-Chagall Collection

This is one of Chagall's first masterpieces. He may have been influenced by some of Bakst's designs for contemporary theatrical productions but the simple yet starkly effective contrast between the white of the dress and the black of the background is very much his own invention. Chagall had begun to discover his own particular style and way of seeing the world. His studies at Saint Petersburg, especially under Leon Bakst, now began to produce distinctive, highly imaginative work. Bakst was one of the men responsible for introducing modern French schools such as Post-Impressionism and Symbolism into Russia.

In 1909, on one of his holidays at Vitebsk, he had met Bella Rosenfeld, Jewish like himself, but from a better-off family. This was the start of their passionate love affair which culminated in their marriage six years later, during the First World War. For as long as she lived, Bella was to be not only Chagall's wife but also his inspiration and his model. Her hair flows down from under her little blue hat; her gloved hands placed so firmly on her hips give her a defiant attitude. Bella is looking into the distance with a deep, rather anxious expression, as if anticipating some of the troubles coming their way. By comparison, the portrait Chagall painted of her 16 years later, *Bella With A Carnation* (centre right), is far less emphatic and forceful.

Double Portrait, 1925 - Oil on canvas, 130 x 94 cm - Paris, private collection. This is one of several double portraits of the artist with Bella, painted when he was achieving great success in Paris. Chagall plays on the contrast between Bella's face in the light and his in partial shadow, on the foreshortening of the canvas, the transparency of the background and the mixture of colours on his palette. These are exactly the same colours as those of the flowers which contrast with the white of his wife's dress.

THE SABBATH

Paris, 1910 - Oil on canvas, 90 x 95 cm
Cologne, Wallraf-Richartz Museum

This was one of the very first paintings Chagall executed after his arrival in Paris in September 1910. In its composition and choice of colours it reveals the powerful influence of Van Gogh, particularly his *Night Cafe - Interior* (below) which was a haunt and a refuge for the drunks and derelicts of Arles, with which Van Gogh was familiar. It is probable that Chagall knew this. He may therefore have been mocking his own stifling, rigidly religious family background here, especially his ever-praying father whom Chagall regarded as absurd. It was only a few weeks since he had arrived in Paris and perhaps too soon for real nostalgia for Russia to emerge in his work.

Certainly this is not a painting which reveals much dignity or religious devotion in the characters depicted. The Sabbath, if studiously enforced, was a time of complete inactivity when no work - not even cooking, theoretically - was permitted. This is presumably the evening of the Sabbath (the candles have been lighted and the clock points to just past ten) and the characters are lolling around slack-bodied, ill-tempered and weak-willed. The strong red colours of the floorboards, repeated in splashes around the walls, increase the atmosphere of disgruntlement and even murderous boredom.

Here, Chagall's palette has the same burning intensity as that of Van Gogh. This painting illustrates Chagall's progress towards his own kind of painting, assimilating both the clashing tones of the Fauvists and the fragmentation of the Cubists. This succeeded in fusing contemporary Paris with the Vitebsk of an earlier period.

This diagram shows the setting of the painting: the plan of the scene, where the perspective is accentuated by the lines of the floorboards, by the background of the wall against which the pendulum of the clock is swinging, and in particular, by the lamplight.

Vincent Van Gogh: Night Cafe - Interior, 1888 - Oil on canvas, 65 x 81 cm - Otterlo, Rijksmuseum Kroller-Muller. The two paintings use a similar setting and choice of colours, but their atmospheres are totally different. In Van Gogh's painting a sense of solitude predominates; while in Chagall's work there is a silent but claustrophobic intimacy.

I AND THE VILLAGE

Paris, 1911 - Oil on canvas, 192 x 151 cm
New York, Museum of Modern Art

This painting is one of the first to show Chagall taking what he needed and wanted from the warring factions of the School of Paris (principally Fauvism and Cubism) and using them to express his own particular vision and dreams. The borrowing from Cubism is particularly evident in the way that conventional three-dimensional perspective has here been completely abandoned for the first time. Instead, he has painted space in a particularly distinctive way, multi-faceted yet not really abstract, even if it bears little relation to external reality. The strong colours show the influence of the Fauvists. But no other artists had painted visions like this.

The surface of the picture is glassy; so too are the forms within it, which are at times positively transparent or crystalline. Visible inside the head of the white cow on the left is another cow being milked, equally white - or possibly it is the same cow. Chagall was deliberately playing with images, juxtaposing and inserting them in a fantastical way, in an attempt to enhance the dream-like atmosphere of the picture, without totally abandoning all aesthetic order.

The order which governs this sort of picture does not derive from ordinary logic but comes almost from another dimension. Chagall has succeeded in resurrecting the world of his Russian childhood - through images of the cows, the church dome and houses of Vitebsk. The magical tree, flowering like something from a fairy tale is held by the green-faced character who is obviously Chagall himself. He took these images, broke them down and juxtaposed them in a manner which echoed that of the Parisian avant-garde. It was these aspects of the Cubist experiment which interested him, following his involvement with Post-Impressionism and Fauvism. However, his poetic Russian soul followed a path very similar to Paul Klee (1879-1940), the Swiss-born painter-poet, or Franz Marc (1880 - 1916), both of whom painted with the lyrical colours of dreams rather than in the self-consciously analytical way of Cubism. This path, in its different forms, sought to cross the threshold of the subconscious. So the fact that the woman who is giving directions to the man with the scythe is actually upside down, as are some of the houses, is perfectly in keeping with the dream-like logic that governs the painting.

Vitebsk, 1908 - Pencil drawing - Artist's collection. A quick sketch drawn in St Petersburg, showing a clear memory of his home-town.

The diagram shows the large circle which seems to be fixed to the cross formed by the diagonals, placed slightly below the centre. Note how the many realistic details of the painting are placed along these diagonals.

TO RUSSIA, ASSES, AND OTHERS

Paris, 1911/12 - Oil on canvas, 156 x 122 cm
Paris, Centre Georges Pompidou

This was one of the first paintings Chagall created during his stay at the artists' colony of La Ruche. Its strange title was suggested by the poet Blaise Cendrars who befriended Chagall, recognising his genius long before rival artists did. It was probably painted in 1912. By this time the artist had finally succeeded in combining all the elements of his distinctive vision, using the superimposition and crossing of planes. This had been derived from his friend Robert Delaunay who had restored colour to Cubism in a distinctively crystalline way, creating a new style called Orphic Cubism.

This picture tells of a dream: nothing in the painting corresponds to the real world outside. In it planes are broken down and recomposed arbitrarily and there is no perspective or depth; we cannot be sure whether it is day or night, but such a point is irrelevant. Geometric figures, luminous stars and animals appear against a dark background. The cow, painted in red, is on a roof; a little man and a calf, both green, crouch beneath it drinking its milk. To one side is the golden dome of a church. A young peasant girl, whose dress is decorated with large peacocks' eyes, is walking in the sky above, her head detached from her body which is striding on. French critics were at a loss to know how to respond when this was exhibited at the Salon des Indépendants in March 1912 but after the First World War the Surrealists claimed this as a forerunner of their movement.

the red sky

the dark sky

the flying head

the woman with the milk bucket

the red cow

the green mannikin

the church

the calf

The sketch separates the individual realistic and fantastic elements which fill the painting, laid out in disarray, or rather in the imaginary "order" of memory and dream. There is obviously some sort of pursuit going on. Chagall clearly intended to mingle reality and imagination in a vision which replaces the sky with the earth. It puts cows on the roofs of houses and a woman in the sky, her head leaving the body in what is less a mystical ascent of the spirit than the tearing apart of the body.

Maternity - 1913 - Oil on canvas, 194 x 115 cm - Amsterdam, Stedelijk Museum. This is another painting in which the figure of a woman floats in a sky where the moon, the birds and a fat goat are mixed together, and where everything seems to be flying. The woman, who is pointing down to the image of a child in her womb, is a symbol of fertility, similar to the mother-figures of antiquity. These sometimes represented the attributes of both sexes: her head reveals a second face on one side, virile and bearded.
She is wearing a dress decorated with scattered flowers, reminiscent of the famous wooden Russian Babushka dolls. The colours are again vibrantly overflowing with life.

PARIS THROUGH THE WINDOW

Paris, 1913 - Oil on canvas, 133 x 140 cm
New York, Guggenheim Museum

Chagall plunged joyfully into the crowds, busy streets and general excitement of Paris "the city of light" when he arrived in 1910, entranced with the splendour of its bright spectacles. Paris at the time seemed the most modern and enjoyable city in the world to almost everybody from eastern Europe, be they the sons of grand dukes or of fishmongers, like Chagall himself. A perceptive delight in Paris is the keynote of this playful yet re-markable work. In the circumstances the appearance of the Eiffel Tower in the background, striding over the streets like a science-fiction monster, is significant both because it symbolises modernity (the Tower was then quite a new edifice) and because it shows his indebtedness to his friend Delaunay, the Orphic Cubist who had recently painted his own version of the Tower. Chagall realised soon after his arrival in the capital that Cubism was the most radical of all the artistic movements, because its breaking-down or decomposition of images and planes allowed the merging or juxtaposition of distant times and places.

This decomposition was useful to him in his interpretation of reality through his own imagination, and his reviving of the world of his earliest memories but in a thoroughly modern form.

In *Paris Through The Window*, he has broken down the planes of the sky, the houses, the Eiffel Tower, the streets, and the window. He has created an arbitrary perspective, an impossible space in which everything becomes possible: a cat with a human face, the two horizontally flying figures outside with their heads pulled towards

each other like magnets, and the upside-down train.

The outer view and the inner visions are perhaps symbolised in the two curiously-coloured faces of the painter in the foreground.

It would be a mistake to try to tie down such an exuberantly imaginative painter as Chagall, by pinning any one artistic label onto him. It was probably this refusal to be pigeon-holed or categorised which accounts both for his initial relative lack of acceptance by most of the other avant-garde painters in Paris and for his enduring popularity with the public since.

The Eiffel Tower shooting up into the sky fascinated Chagall and it often features in his paintings. It was a symbol of Paris and, above all, a symbol of the new artistic vision which Paris gave to the artist. In Memory Of Paris 1976 - Oil on canvas, 73 x 54 cm - Artist's collection, the planes of light and colours (green, red, orange, yellow, blue and violet: the colours of the spectrum) have been broken down, and the tower and the opera house loom up next to the lovers.

DOUBLE PORTRAIT WITH WINE GLASS

Vitebsk, 1917 - Oil on canvas, 233 x 136 cm
Paris, Centre Georges Pompidou

This great double portrait, along with *The Birthday* (below) and *The Promenade*, belongs to the series of paintings which celebrate the painter's love for Bella, whom he had married at last in 1915. It was painted during the First World War, when Chagall was mainly in Vitebsk. During the first years of his enforced stay in Russia (1914-23) Chagall had been overwhelmed by seeing again at first hand the motifs which had fuelled his art in Paris - houses, cows, roofs, and the Jewish people amongst whom he had lived as a child. He had painted them repeatedly, always with the same fantastic, visionary eye but now with a calmer, more classical style. This was less because of the new artistic movements he heard about in Moscow - principally Suprematism, a form of dogmatic

This diagram shows the vertical structure of the composition and the strange impression of swaying, almost of intoxication, created by the slight incline in the couple's stance. The shape of the canvas is very elongated to provide space for their soaring flight, and for their joy which soars above earthly concerns. To emphasise the euphoria of the moment, in which a toast is being drunk to pure happiness, Chagall has slightly inclined the axis of the composition, the ideal line which crosses the figures, causing the lovers to stagger. Bella's feet do not rest on the ground, but float above the water. The joyful couple are backed by the panorama of Vitebsk, here more realistically depicted than earlier.

The Birthday , 1915 - Oil on canvas, 81 x 98 cm - New York, Museum of Modern Art. Another love scene with Chagall soaring above, kissing Bella and encircling her in his flight. Of this painting, Bella recalled: "Through the windows a cloud and a patch of blue sky called to us. The brightly hung walls whirled around us. We flew over fields of flowers, shuttered houses, roofs, yards, churches. The walls, decorated with multicoloured shawls, ripple around us and make us turn our heads."

abstract art pioneered by Kasimir Malevich - than through the logic of his own inner development. The influence of his friend the French Cubist Robert Delaunay is still apparent in its vertical format, which was inspired by Delaunay's painting *The Eiffel Tower*. Delaunay shared Chagall's love of colour. However, there is less Cubist fragmentation of form here than in some of his previous paintings. This is due to the influence of classical art, especially Renaissance masters such Giotto, Piero della Francesca and Masaccio, whose art he had been studying in books during his enforced semi-idleness in Vitebsk. But it is the couple's almost ecstatic happiness which gives this canvas an unreal charm typical of Chagall. Bella presumably did not carry her husband around on her shoulders while he waved a wine glass in the air and an angel shot past above.

On the left are the pale tones of the sky, while on the right are large planes of yellow. The green of his waistcoat under his red jacket (a harmony of complementary colours which enhance each other and which are heightened by the presence of the white) accentuates the splendour of the colours. All this increases the feeling of joy which emanates from one of the happiest of Chagall's paintings, and perhaps one of the happiest in western art.

In this painting Chagall seems to have delighted in small visual tricks, such as angling his head to make it look almost dislocated, to emphasise their happiness. Similarly, the artist has placed one hand over his wife's eye in a playful gesture, whilst she clutches a multi-coloured fan.

THE GREEN VIOLINIST

Paris, 1923 - Oil on canvas, 196 x 108 cm
New York, Guggenheim Museum

The image or archetype of the fiddler or violinist recurred throughout Chagall's long life and art, from very early versions such as that of 1912, painted in Paris and exhibited in 1914, to late versions such as *The Purple Violinist* (below). Music had been the one art accepted in the generally philistine household of Chagall's youth and Chagall himself could play the violin. His uncle Neuch had also often played the violin, and travelling violinists were part of the main ceremonial occasions in the lives of the Jewish community in Russia: births, marriages and deaths. These were such vivid and intense memories that he painted them constantly.

The Green Violinist takes up the theme of a wall painting, created in 1920 for the Jewish Theatre of the same central figure surrounded by houses, a fence, a tree with a bird, and a ladder; a ladder is the motif which symbolises upward movement in Chagall's painting. The musician's face is a brilliant green, as are his hands, while his coat and cap are a resplendent violet. Such unreal touches are typical of Chagall's art, as is the animal with a large muzzle in the foreground, the little man who is holding his violin by the neck and finally the figure floating in the air - a motif so common in Chagall's art it could almost be called a trademark. Chagall returned to Paris in 1923 after an absence of nine years. This piece which was produced in the same year, was probably his last work painted in Russia.

The Purple Violinist, *1967 - Oil on canvas, 43 x 43 cm - Private collection. This may be a painting of his uncle playing in the snow beneath the moon, or perhaps it is of one of the itinerant violinists who turned up for festivals. Once again, Chagall has combined fantastic colours, such as violet and green, against the white background of the snow-bound village. The village is more realistically depicted than in* The Green Violinist *but there is still a fantastic touch - a chicken playing the violin, on the left.*

Two pen and ink drawings of the same subject, but treated in different ways. The first, The Jew Playing The Violin *(top, Artist's collection), uses only outlines to evoke the characteristics of the subject's personality, and is reminiscent of Matisse's drawings. Barely-defined details, such as the hand and the violin, bring the whole together and invite the beholder to use imagination to complete the drawing. The second drawing,* The Violinist *(1911, Private collection), is a unique work in its balance and play of light and dark.*

THE LOVERS' BOUQUET

Maurillon, 1926 - Oil on canvas, 92 x 73 cm
Venice, Private collection

On his return to Paris in 1923, Chagall soon established himself as one of the most popular painters in the Modern movement. This was mainly due to the lyrical beauty of his style, especially his original and vivid colouring, and the potent appeal of his dream-like images. The 1920s saw a general revival of interest in classical art, which affected painters as different in their aims as Matisse and Picasso. Chagall, although never a follower of either, was also affected by this trend. He abandoned the quasi-Cubist multiple viewpoints of some of his earlier works in favour of a rather more straightforward figurative approach.

But this picture remains quintessentially Chagall. The lovers, clasping one another so fondly on the right, the Russian village so splendidly out of scale behind them with its outsize chickens and yellow violin, the enormous bunch of flowers with its huge white lilies soaring out of an allotment - all could only come from the world, midway between a remembered dream and reality, which Chagall had made his own.

The Fiancée, With Flowers, 1926 - Oil on board, 59 x 46 cm - Rome, Private collection. Love and flowers: the fiancée, or rather the wife, dressed in white, is seen among the white patches of the flowers which lighten the background. Here, the green, the violet, the red and the blue all blend together. In the big bouquet, the young woman seems to be floating as if in a dream.

Two Lovers With An Angel - Pen and ink drawing, 22 x 15 cm - Switzerland, Private collection. The lovers have clearly been transported to heaven, above everyday earthly events; it is therefore reasonable that they should meet an angel. The faint lines of the artist are enough to create a face and a kiss.

The diagram shows the "space" of the painting taken up by the huge bouquet of flowers, and that in which the lovers are holding each other.

EQUESTRIENNE

Paris, 1927 - Oil on canvas, 100 x 81 cm
Prague, Narodni Galerie

Chagall was busy creating the illustrations for La Fontaine's *Fables*, started in 1926, when the art dealer Vollard suggested a new project: a series based on the theme of the circus. They both went to the Cirque d'Hiver (Winter Circus), where Chagall, like so many others, was fascinated by the magic of the show. It reminded him of his childhood, in which the world of men and the world of animals intermingled. The *Equestrienne* of 1927 is partly a tribute to the circus.

This was a very happy period of his life, when he was frequenting theatres and concerts and enjoying the fashionable side of Parisian life. This enjoyment shines through this delightful work, whose decorative aspects again recall some of the contemporary works of Matisse. The dress of the young woman clasping her horse in a most acrobatic gesture, resembles a bouquet of flowers formed from a mass of small touches of colour. The horse itself is a mass of colour, with blues predominating. On the right, just visible, a violinist once again adds a musical accompaniment. Here, the circus represents grace and harmony above all; the circus rider and the horse seem united in their elegant, improbable motion. The animal's adornments and the woman's costume merge in a harmony of cold colours: blues, greens, and light blues.

Chagall's preparatory studies for illustrating La Fontaine's *Fables* made him more familiar with animals, and so renewed his love for them - a love which dated from early childhood in his village which was full of animals. They were to become perhaps more evident than before in his imaginary world, almost becoming the main subjects.

The Circus Rider, *1931 - Oil on canvas, 100 x 81 cm - Amsterdam, Stedelijk Museum. Here Chagall has added the theme of the circus to that of his favourite - lovers embracing - and treated it with elegance and sophistication. The only bright colour is that of the circus rider's dress and the fan.*

Acrobat With Green Bouquet, *1953 - Indian ink and wax crayon, 60 x 30 cm - Paris, Galerie Maeght. Once again, after 30 years, Chagall returned to the circus and all its dramas. The acrobat's circular movement is emphasised by the inclusion (yet again!) of a bouquet of flowers.*

At The Circus, *1976 - Oil on canvas, 109 x 122 cm - Artist's collection. This painting is characterised by the beam of yellow light which crosses the scene and lights up the acrobat and the horse, two yellow marks against the violet and blue of the crowd of spectators.*

TO MY WIFE

New York, 1944 - Oil on canvas, 131 x 194 cm
Paris, Centre Georges Pompidou

This is the second version of a piece painted 11 years earlier. Bella died suddenly on 2 September 1944 after a brief viral illness. Chagall was devastated and this painting, a memorial to her, relates the events of their life together.

The composition is divided vertically into two parts. On the left Chagall and his wife are shown on the day of their wedding, beneath a ceremonial red canopy. On the right, Bella is lying naked on a reddish-orange bed, with a vase overflowing with a bouquet of flowers behind her; high above her a multi-coloured goat or donkey holds a three-branched candelabra. Above her, on the grey curtain, he has written the inscription A MA FEMME (To My Wife).

Every part of this picture is thought to be richly symbolic, although not always easy to interpret. The fish holding an umbrella in the bottom left corner is thought to represent the depths of the sea (and so of the human soul); next to it the cock, a recurrent image in Chagall's work, symbolises the sun and spiritual energies. The clock in the centre registers and gloomily records and emphasises passing time. The red angel in the left corner may be

Azrael, the Jewish angel of death, here come to collect Bella's soul. Besides these often sombre symbols there are many more cheerful references to their lives together, especially the circus scenes on the left and the village scenes in the background. Some touches, such as the violinist, recur in almost all of his works at this time.

Time Is A River Without Banks, 1939 - Oil on canvas, 103 x 83 cm - New York, Museum of Modern Art. The title reveals the symbolism of the painting. The Surrealists claimed Chagall as one of their school because of this type of painting.

This sketch shows the two parts of the composition: the couple on one hand, and on the other, the chaste and delicate nude of Bella which stands out in its limpidity against the oranges and reds of the coverlet. The whole painting is framed like a great stage set.

THE SOUL OF THE CITY

New York, 1945 - Oil on canvas, 106 x 82 cm
Paris, Centre Georges Pompidou

This great painting, dating from the very end of the Second World War, incorporates all the grief Chagall felt at this time, when Bella was dead and his universe looked utterly bleak.

The image of crucifixion is central to this picture. Chagall, although brought up as a Hasidic Jew, had long ago rejected his father's ritualistic devotions and for a time seemed content to live without any overtly religious faith. The impact of the Second World War, and especially the Nazi murder of six million fellow Jews, rekindled his consciousness of Judaism, but in an unorthodox form. In particular, he seized upon the image of the Crucifixion to produce images of suffering relevant to all mankind - and not just to Christians. In the 1930s and 1940s he painted many Crucifixions such as *The White Crucifixion* (right).

Here the artist is shown as a young man, reaching up to the painting of the crucifix with his left hand and his left face while with his right (a typical Chagall device, this double visage) he looks down on the ghostly form of Bella in her white wedding dress. She is stretched across the canvas, from the tabernacle of the Torah to the purifying fire of the candle flames in the candelabra in the bottom left. In the background is Vitebsk once again with a sleigh riding in the sky - another aerial trademark.

The tones reflect the state of mind of the artist whose violet jacket stands out against the predominant grey-green-blue of the painting, brightened by the yellow touches of the crucifix, the red of the tabernacle's curtain, the blue of the animals and above all, the white of Bella's image.

The White Crucifixion, 1938 - Oil on canvas - 155 x 140 cm - Chicago, The Art Institute. The crucifix here symbolises not the Christian Saviour, but the martyred Jewish people; Christ is portrayed explicitly as Jewish. Like the Christ in The Soul Of The City, a piece of the prayer shawl, with its double black stripe, is wrapped around his hips. All around, scenes of havoc and violence against his people are in evidence. A storm trooper bursts into a burning synagogue in the right background while a Torah burns in the right foreground and further scenes of anti-semitic violence fill the left.

The tabernacle of the Torah, topped with the lions of Judah and the Tables of the Law, is present in both these paintings. In The Soul Of The City it is connected to the figure of Bella in her wedding dress, to emphasise the link of

woman with the traditions of the Jewish people. In The White Crucifixion, it is in the midst of the flames destroying the synagogue, in front of which there is a Nazi soldier. The image is yet another symbolising Jewish martyrdom.

THE LOVERS IN THE SKY ABOVE VENCE

Vence, 1956-60 - Oil on canvas, 131 x 98 cm
Private collection

At the unveiling of his decorations for the ceiling of the Opéra de Paris in 1964, Chagall announced that he had wanted to put the dreams and creations of the performers and musicians up above, as a crowning piece; that he had wanted to sing like a bird, without being restrained by theory or method.

Chagall's last pieces were indeed fed by an even freer sense of imagination than before, more ethereal and dream-like. When Chagall moved to Vence in 1950, in the strong Mediterranean light so dear to Cézanne, Picasso, Matisse and other great artists, his palette was enriched by deeper tones and personal maturity.

In *The Lovers In The Sky Above Vence*, there is clearly a return to the subjects he favoured in his youth: above all, the emotions of love, the obsessive and recurrent theme of his whole life. Here, the painting is far from the Cubist influence of his youth, when Chagall used the crossing and super-imposition of planes to enter a dream-like dimension where time and place lost their boundaries to weave new ones. However, space still lacks depth and perspective, and is abstract and fantastic, unifying the diverse elements in the transparency of an atmosphere where the objects and people are weightless. They float, transformed by love and imagination into a "bouquet of dreams".

The lovers are stretched along the diagonal, the left-hand side of which is transparent against the the blue background of the sky and the Mediterranean landscape; to the right are the colours of an extraordinary bouquet of flowers in yellows, reds, blues, whites and violets, which are lit up by the candelabra. The moon behind the stems also seems to be a flower, lighting up the markedly evanescent faces of the characters with its beams.

The diagram illustrates the composition of the painting, based on the downward sloping diagonal which crosses it from left to right. On one side, there is the loving couple, swaying across the canvas. On the other side of the diagonal is the great vase of flowers which explodes like a firework of colours.

Bouquet Of Flowers And The Blue Village, *1959 - Oil on canvas, 78 x 71 cm - Paris, Galerie Maeght. Another bouquet of flowers and another loving couple. However, this time it is the red of the flowers in the foreground which plays the most important part. The blue figures stand out against the village in the background, and are surrounded by a mysterious atmosphere.*

THE MAGICAL REALIST

Chagall left his birthplace of Vitebsk, a small country town, when he was 20. From then on, apart from five years when the First World War kept him there once again, he travelled the world, often living in its great cities from Moscow to New York. He became in the end a celebrity and a world figure comparable to Picasso or Matisse. Due to the formative years he spent in Paris, he is generally labelled as belonging to the School of Paris - a label wide enough to include such differing talents as Braque and Modigliani. Yet, although Chagall spent most of his life in France, being finally accepted by the French establishment, his art remains hard to classify, except as that of a "primitive" painter. Indeed, his themes have more in common with the poetic fantasies of Germanic painters like Paul Klee or Franz Marc than with the consciously intellectual works of most French painters.

Above all, it was the memories of his Vitebsk childhood, recalled so vividly and so originally, which were always to provide his main inspiration. In fact, Chagall, working

CHAGALL AND HIS TIMES

	HIS LIFE AND WORKS	HISTORY	ART AND CULTURE
1887	Born on 7 July in Vitebsk in Russia	Foundation of the Indo-Chinese Union Italians crushingly defeated at Doughali by the Ethiopians	Van Gogh starts his *Sunflower* series Seurat exhibits *La Grande Jatte* at the Salon of XX in Brussels
1907	Moves to St Petersburg to study at the Imperial School	New Zealand becomes a self-governing dominion Rasputin establishes dominance over Russian Imperial Court	Picasso: *Les Demoiselles D'Avignon* Birth of W.H. Auden Rudyard Kipling wins the Nobel Prize for literature
1909	Studies with Leon Bakst in Saint Petersburg, returning to Vitebsk where he meets Bella Rosenfeld, who becomes his fiancee	Blériot makes first cross-Channel flight House of Lords rejects Lloyd George's budget, starting constitutional crisis in Britain	Gustav Klimt: *Judith (II)* Matisse: *The Dance* Birth of Francis Bacon
1910	Leaves for Paris, where he paints *The Sabbath*	Death of Edward VII; Accession of George V Liberals win two General Elections	E.M. Forster: *Howard's End* Death of Henri Rousseau Fernand Léger: *Nude In The Forest* Igor Stravinksy: *The Firebird*
1911	Exhibits at the Salon des Indépendants, where he gets to know Apollinaire and Blaise Cendrars. Paints *To Russia, Asses And Others, I And The Village*	Parliament Act greatly reduces powers of House of Lords Amundsen reaches South Pole before Captain Scott Italians seize Libya from Turks	Max Beerbohm: *Zuleika Dobson* Walter Sickert founds the Camden Town Group of painters H.G. Wells: *The New Machiavelli*
1914	Personal exhibition at Der Sturm Gallery in Berlin. Visits Vitebsk and is trapped by the outbreak of war	Assassination of Archduke Ferdinand at Sarajevo starts First World War; Germans invade Belgium and France but repelled at the Marne; start of trench warfare Russian invasion of Germany defeated at Battle of Tannenberg	James Joyce: *Portrait Of The Artist As A Young Man* Renoir: *Seated Nude* André Gide: *The Vatican Cellars*
1915	Marries Bella Rosenfeld; exhibits at Moscow	Italy enters the war on the Allied side British attack on Dardanelles fails disastrously	T.S. Eliot: *Prufrock And Other Observations* Virginia Woolf: *The Voyage Out* D.H. Lawrence: *The Rainbow*
1918	Is made Commissar for the Arts for Vitebsk, becomes director of the Academy	Treaty of Brest Litovsk: Russia cedes immense territories to Germany; start of Russian Civil War Armistice; collapse of Germany	Death of Apollinaire and Klimt James Joyce: *Exiles* Lytton Strachey: *Eminent Victorians*
1920	Dismissed from the Vitebsk Academy, moves to Moscow. Paints scenery for the Jewish Theatre	First meeting of the League of Nations End of the Russo-Polish war Prohibition starts in the USA	Paul Klee joins the Bauhaus Marcel Proust: *Le Côté De Guermantes* D. H. Lawrence: *The Lost Girl*
1923	Returns to Paris via Berlin. Agrees to illustrate books for Vollard. Paints *The Green Violinist*	Hitler's Beer-Hall Putsch in Munich fails French armies occupy German Ruhr	Sigmund Freud: *The Ego And The Id* H.G. Wells: *Men Like Gods* Lutyens building New Delhi
1931	Visits Palestine. Publishes *My Life*	Proclamation of a republic in Spain Great Depression at its worst	Virginia Woolf: *The Waves* William Walton: *Belshazzar's Feast*

through the most flamboyantly progressive and iconoclastic decades ever known in Western art, was forever looking backward, with a visionary nostalgia almost as powerful as that of Marcel Proust, the novelist. In his autobiography *Ma Vie* of 1931, he wrote that all his imagery, no matter how bizarre, derived directly from reminiscences of his early years.

Chagall grew up in a semi-rural world; Jews in the western parts of Russia at the beginning of the century were often farmers, not townspeople, and it is rustic images - of cocks, cows, goats or sheep - which recur throughout Chagall's work. This distinguishes his art from the dominant themes of Modernism, which concerned itself primarily with the city

and urban life. But he also grew up a devout Jew, attending synagogue services and reading the Torah. Judaism's prohibition of imagery, coupled with the extremely limited intellectual horizons of Chagall's family and friends, meant that he had few immediate examples of real merit as painters before he went to Saint Petersburg in 1907.

1941	Leaves for the United States after France is overrun by the Nazis	Greece invaded by Germany Germany attacks Russia Pearl harbour; surprise attack by Japanese on US naval base brings America into war	Death of James Joyce and Virginia Woolf Herbert Marcuse: *Reason And Revolution* Renato Guttuso: *Crucifixion*
1944	Death of Bella. *To My Wife*	Allied landings in Normandy and liberation of Paris German offensive in the Ardennes fails Warsaw uprising crushed	Bertold Brecht: *Schweik In The Second World War* Louis Macneice: *Springboard* Death of Lutyens and Kandinsky
1950	Settles in Vence. Starts making ceramics. Exhibition at the Zurich Kunsthaus	Start of the Korean War China invades Tibet	Ionesco: *The Bald Prima Donna* Death of George Bernard Shaw Stanley Spencer: *Resurrection, Port Glasgow*
1952	Marries Valentine Brodsky. Journeys to Greece and Italy	George VI dies; accession of Elizabeth II Britain explodes its first atomic bomb West Germany becomes an independent nation	Dylan Thomas: *Collected Poems* Ernest Hemingway: *The Old Man And The Sea* Samuel Beckett: *Waiting For Godot*
1958	Produces scenery and costumes for Ravel's ballet *Daphnis And Chloe*	End of the Fourth Republic in France due to Algerian crisis; De Gaulle becomes President EEC established Iraqi monarchy overthrown	Harold Pinter: *The Birthday Party* Juan Miró decorates the UNESCO building in Paris Samuel Beckett: *Krapp's Last Tape*
1964	Visits New York. Starts new decorative scheme for the Paris Opéra ceilings commissioned by De Gaulle	Death of Nehru in India Nelson Mandela imprisoned for life in South Africa Labour leader Wilson wins General Election	Philip Larkin: *The Whitsun Weddings* Saul Bellow: *Herzog* Death of Georges Braque
1966	Starts work on great decorative murals for the New York Opera; settles in Saint-Paul-de-Vence	Indira Gandhi becomes premier of India Start of the Cultural Revolution in China Wilson wins General Election with increased majority	Death of Evelyn Waugh Tom Stoppard: *Rosencrantz and Guildenstern Are Dead*
1973	Opening of the National Marc Chagall Museum at Nice, where he designs the stained glass for the concert hall	Britain joins the EEC Watergate scandal in US reveals Nixon's criminality Allende government overthrown in Argentina by Fascist coup OPEC quadruples oil price	Death of W.H. Auden Federico Fellini: *Amarcord* Iris Murdoch: *The Black Prince*
1977	Exhibits at the Louvre	Queen Elizabeth's Silver Jubilee Military coup in Pakistan overthrows Bhutto's elected government	Opening of the Georges Pompidou Centre Tom Stoppard: *Every Good Boy Deserves Favour*
1985	Dies 28 March in Saint-Paul-de-Vence	Gorbachev becomes leader of Soviet Union Greenpeace ship blown up by French secret service in New Zealand	Death of Philip Larkin Woody Allen: *The Purple Rose Of Cairo*

There, in the studio of Bakst, he encountered only at second-hand the works of the Post-Impressionists, especially Gauguin, and other French schools. Bakst himself was primarily a stage designer, temperamentally too different from Chagall to serve as a really illuminating teacher. Chagall effectively had to create his own style as a painter even more than most painters. This self-development, although it might have been a crippling limitation, meant that all the contending art forms he would encounter never totally overwhelmed him, nor diverted him from following his own path. This proved singularly appropriate for a painter whose primary concerns would always be depicting his world of memories, dreams and magic. Yet it took the experience of Paris, and its distance from his Russian roots, to enable his art to mature so suddenly.

Paris in 1910 was in an extraordinary state of artistic ferment. The Fauvists had startled the art world five years earlier with their violent colours, first exhibited at the Salon d'Automne; more recently and even more radically the Cubists, led by Picasso and Braque, had begun their disintegration of form. Chagall, in his first months, however, sidestepped current trends to marvel mainly at the old masters in the Louvre. Delacroix, Veronese, Poussin and Rembrandt, along with more recent painters such as Manet, opened his eyes to a far wider range of painting than he had seen in Russia. Wandering through the art galleries of famous dealers like Durand Ruel and Vollard allowed him also to see at first hand the works of Cézanne, Van Gogh and Gauguin.

THE CUBIST EXAMPLE

In 1912 Chagall rented a tiny room in the artists' colony of La Ruche. Here he worked alongside many other artistic exiles such as Amadeo Modigliani and Chaim Soutine (1893-1943), who was also of Russian-Jewish origin. Inspired by the hyper-febrile atmosphere of this ramshackle yet teeming building, Chagall began painting his dream-like pictures. Almost all of these Paris paintings looked back to his childhood for their themes but drew on the latest artistic developments for their form.

Cubism - more particularly, the branch of Cubism called Orphic Cubism pioneered by his new friend Robert Delaunay, which had restored crystalline colours to the monochrome art of Picasso - came to Chagall's aid in one vital way at this time. By following the Cubist fragmentation and overlapping of different planes (*plans superposés*), Chagall was able to superimpose different planes to suggest different psychic levels; each transparent plane in his pictures corresponded to a level of memory or dream, all co-existing simultaneously on the canvas.

This is already apparent in *I And The Village* (page 8) of 1911. It is even stronger in *To Russia, Asses And Others* of 1912 (page 10) and *Paris Through the Window* (page 12). Normal depth and dimensions have been jettisoned to enhance the dream-like, magical atmosphere which the poet André Breton would later hail as a precursor of Surrealism. Delaunay's influence is again obvious in *Double Portrait With Wine Glass* (pages 14-17), whose vertical format and toppling forms of Chagall and Bella owe much to Delaunay's *The City Of Paris.*

Chagall later dismissed the Surrealists' claims, just as he distanced himself from the further, all-too-logical developments of Cubism. "Let them choke themselves on their square pears or their triangular tables," he wrote in his autobiography. "My art is an extravagant art, a flaming vermilion, a blue soul flooding over my paintings." If Chagall was happy to use the means of Orphic Cubism whilst evolving his own style, he never pursued Cubist ends. Instead, he remained faithful to his world of dreams - a far more spontaneously unconscious world than the often laboured one of the Surrealists. Once he had found the means he needed to express this inner world, his art changed relatively little. Perhaps this is not so surprising; the world of the unconscious, as Freud pointed out, is timeless and changeless. So, too, was the essence of Chagall's art.

HASIDIC MYSTICISM

It has been suggested that Chagall's works owe their distinctive quality of simultaneity to Russian icons, which also figured many different actions occurring in one painting at the same time. But a more probable and certainly more accessible source for Chagall must have been the Hasidic Jewish tradition. This saw the entire world as filled to overflowing with divine mysteries; every creature, every object, contained a latent spark of the divine which could be awakened by religion - or by art. The miraculous lurked in every corner, just under the surface of daily life. Hasidic teachings presented an image of God's love flowing over into the world, where it was shattered into a million fragments which could be retrieved by men.

Chagall did not like too much emphasis being laid on religious aspects of his art. But this near-mystical, half-magical approach recurs in his work from *Self-Portrait With Seven Fingers* of 1913 (page 1) to the more serious religious element of *The Soul Of The City* (page 26). Its crucified Jew (on the canvas), an extremely unorthodox image which he repeated many times, reveals his empathy with the sufferings of his people.

His last works, however, were peaceful, even idyllic. *Lovers In The Sky Above Vence* (page 28) may feature a seven-branched Jewish candlestick but its image of almost heavenly bliss transcends religious divisions. Here again the lessons learnt long ago in Paris enable him to disregard limitations of space and planes to create a celestial, softly coloured tapestry. The landscape is no longer that of Vitebsk but of southern France, where so many painters, from Renoir to Picasso, had ended their careers. At the end of his long life, Chagall seemed no longer in painful exile from his Russian home but reconciled and at peace.

Self-Portrait, 1506
Oil on canvas,
45 x 33 cm
Florence, Uffizi
Gallery

RAPHAEL

"His spirit spreads absolute order everywhere, and a harmony which sings."
Eugène Delacroix, 1830

Raphael was born in the duchy of Urbino in central Italy on Good Friday in 1483. The great biographer of the Renaissance artists, Vasari, attached great importance to the actual day of Raphael's birth, Good Friday - the day of the Crucifixion. Partly inspired by this apparently divine connection, he considered Raphael's art to be almost heavenly in its perfection. Remarkably good-looking, sweet-tempered and courteous, Raphael seemed to sit in a golden glow on the summit of the High Renaissance (1500-1520), flanked by Leonardo and Michelangelo.

This attitude soon became universal; it dominated views of the artist for centuries. Then there came a violent reaction against Raphael's fame in the mid-19th century. From being hailed as superhumanly perfect, he came to be thought sweet, insipid, even kitsch. Neither view does justice to such a vital, powerful artist.

Raphael, properly called Raffaello Sanzio, was the son of Giovanni di Sante di Pietro Sanzio, a minor painter and writer, and of Magia di Battista. His father, who was attached to the ducal court, died when Raphael was 11; his

mother had died three years earlier. Raphael was left in the care of his uncle; more importantly, he was apprenticed to Pietro Perugino in Perugia.

At the end of the 15th century, Perugino was the most popular and prolific painter in central Italy. During the 1490s, he was constantly travelling between Florence and Perugia, producing paintings on spiritual subjects, with smooth-browed saints and sweet-faced madonnas of a repetitively gentle piety. But the spatial clarity and idealised figures of his works shaped Raphael's early art.

Raphael's native Urbino was one of the smallest but most cultured of the Italian states. Under its dukes Federigo and Guidobaldo, its court became one of the most civilised in Europe. In the early 16th century Baldassare Castiglione set his famous book *The Courtier* there; later Raphael would paint his equally famous portrait of this writer, diplomat, courtier and true Renaissance man (page 26). If Raphael started in Perugino's shadow, he soon outstripped him as *The Marriage Of The Virgin* (page 4) of 1504 already shows, with its far surer command of depth and volume than Perugino could

manage. 1504 was also the year that Raphael first arrived in Florence, armed with a letter from the sister of the duchess of Urbino, Giovanna Feltria della Rovere: "The bearer of this letter will be Raphael, a painter from Urbino, very successful in his business... he is a quiet, courteous young man. I am very fond of him..." Despite this letter, Raphael did not receive any public commissions. But staying in Florence enabled him to get to know artists such as Leonardo, Michelangelo and Fra Bartolommeo, all then in Florence.

Raphael was interested in everything and everyone. From Leonardo he learned the technique of giving figures volume and weight in space and the blending of colours, from Michelangelo how to produce a dynamic and heroically muscular quality and from Fra Bartolommeo he discovered how to endow his figures with majesty and grandeur. Also, more importantly, he saw at first hand the notorious competition between the two acknowledged masters of the time, Leonardo and Michelangelo, to decorate different walls of the Sala del Consiglio in the Palazzo della Signoria with huge frescoes depicting the battles of Anghiari and Cascina. The full impact of such violent, dramatic movement,

which seemed to glorify violent clashes of very muscular figures and was totally new to Raphael, was not to be reflected in his art until he reached Rome but his *Saint George And The Dragon* of 1505 (page 8) shows Leonardo's violently lunging horse. Similarly, the very agitated characters in *The Entombment* of 1507 (page 12) reveal Michelangelo's influence.

More typical of Raphael, however, are the Madonnas he painted during his years in Florence, such as *The Madonna Of The Goldfinch* (page 14). This, while retaining all the sweetness of a Perugino madonna, has a monumentality, depth, and colour clearly derived from his recent studies. In particular, Leonardo's landscapes are echoed in Raphael's background. But Raphael gave his Holy Families a far more serene, healthy and harmonious atmosphere than the rather sinister canvases of Leonardo.

The young painter's fame must have spread surprisingly widely for in 1508 he was summoned to Rome by Pope Julius II. Julius wanted to transform the still ramshackle city into the true capital of Christendom, eclipsing the ruined grandeurs of antiquity with new Christian buildings. Accordingly, the great architect Bramante

Drawing by Raphael for an engraving of The Massacre Of The Innocents by Raimondi, c. 1510 - Windsor, Royal Library

was summoned to replace the ancient Saint Peter's with a modern cathedral; Michelangelo was commissioned to transform the Sistine Chapel and a group of painters, among them the young Raphael, was assembled to decorate Julius' personal apartments. Raphael revealed himself so superior to his rivals that he was soon given control of the decorative schemes.

The frescoes in the first of these rooms, known as the Stanza della Segnatura, were based on a complicated theological programme explaining the harmony and continuity between pagan

Angel With Raised Arms, c.1510 - Drawing for the cartoon of one the mosaics for the Chigi Chapel of St Mary of the People, Rome

Greek philosophy and Christian doctrine. On one wall, in *The School Of Athens,* (pages 18-22) the ancient philosophers, led by Plato and Aristotle, debate in an immense architectural setting. On the opposite wall, in *The Disputà* (page 16), theologians discuss the mysteries of the Catholic faith below while above the Trinity is surrounded by saints, martyrs and angels, set in a luminous open space. The lyrical monumentality of both pictures shows Raphael widening his powers immensely and has been tremendously influential on western art ever since.

After its completion in 1511, Raphael was entrusted with three other apartments, in the first of which, the Stanza di Eliodoro, he painted *The Liberation Of Saint Peter* (page 24), and *The Expulsion Of Heliodorus From The Temple* (page 21). In 1517 the last Room was completed in which his assistants' collaboration is clearly visible. Some, like Giulio Romano, later became major painters.

Raphael had by now become the most famous in Rome, working for clients like the wealthy Sienese banker Agostino Chigi as well as the Church. For Chigi he did the wonderful fresco of *Galatea* (page 22) without delegating it. This shows his complete mastery of mythologies and, more importantly, his final definition of an ideal of female beauty. Later, he completed the Loggia di Psiche in the Villa Farnesina and the Logge Vaticane; these were such immense projects that Raphael, now overwhelmed with work, was only able to supervise their execution.

Raphael's charm, elegance and good looks were legendary. Vasari talks of his "amorous excesses", but these are undocumented; he did paint a portrait of a woman, *La Fornarina,* who may have been one of his mistresses. Vasari also described Raphael as "so gentle and kind that even animals loved him."

In 1513 Pope Leo X had confirmed his predecessor's appreciation of Raphael by appointing him Superintendent of Roman Antiquities - a post Raphael took very seriously, striving to preserve Rome's great ruins from those who regarded them as quarries. He also branched out into architecture (as did many Renaissance artists), taking over from Bramante at Saint Peter's in 1514.

Raphael's last years were frantically busy in many fields. His portrait of the pleasure-loving pontiff Leo X (page 26) is a masterpiece of unsycophantic observation, while that of Baldassare Castiglione (page 26) is deeply sympathetic and one of the seminal portraits of Western art. Finally, in *The Transfiguration* (page 28), he seems to be moving away from pure classicism as if he had already exhausted its possibilities.

Far more certainly, he was exhausting himself. He was very sociable and mingled with the nobility of Rome on equal terms in the evening, while working all day. Such a combination proved fatal; on Good Friday, 1520, "that most gentle and excellent of painters" died. Appropriately, he was buried in the Pantheon - the noble Roman temple, transformed into a church, which he had so admired.

Drawing of the interior of the Pantheon showing the Chigi Chapel of St Mary of the People, which he designed and built about 1515

THE MARRIAGE OF THE VIRGIN

Detail - 1504 - Oil on panel, 170 x 117 cm
Milan, Pinacoteca di Brera

This is one of the first pictures which shows the young Raphael completely outstripping his master Perugino, although the influence of the older painter is still evident, especially in the architectural motifs. These recall those used by Perugino in *Christ Giving The Keys To Saint Peter* (1482, Sistine Chapel, Rome) and, more obviously, his own *Marriage Of The Virgin* (1499). Commissioned by the Abezzini family for the chapel of Saint Joseph in Citta di Castello, this is clearly signed (above the temple entrance) and dated 1504. Raphael's use of perspective here is overwhelming.

The open door of the building, meant to be the Temple of Jerusalem, serves as the vanishing point (that point at which two seemingly parallel lines in a picture would meet) for the strong pattern of the pavement. Raphael, unlike his master, has made his figures the same size as the building, thereby giving his painting greater unity. Perugino's figures stand in a linear arrangement, the two halves of the picture sharply separated by the stiff figure of the high priest in the centre. In Raphael's, by contrast, the priest inclines his head and turns gently towards the Virgin,

who has a lyrical grace never equalled by Perugino. Joseph stands in a totally natural, easy manner, showing Raphael, still only 20, surpassing Perugino in the realistic yet idealised style which became the hallmark of the High Renaissance. This was something Perugino could never master. There are still strong elements of the more stylised 15th century manner, however, especially in the golden light diffused throughout the picture. Even the temple, set against a clear blue sky so typical of the central Italian school, seems to have been dipped in gold.

The elegant building, centrally positioned, dominates the upper half of the canvas. It is not simply a background architectural element, it is also an airy and noble edifice in its own right. It is almost circular with its 16 sides, sited at the top of a flight of steps at the end of the perspective created by the paving. Raphael, emerging from the influence of Perugino, brought his critical intelligence to this aspect of pictorial space, which Leonardo and Bramante, the greatest architect of the High Renaissance, had studied already. Even in this early picture, the stirrings of Raphael the Roman architect can be discerned.

The diagram shows the structure of the perspective, converging towards the vanishing point at the centre of the picture and the entrance of the building. This centre coincides with the apex of the triangle which contains the main figures. The diagram also shows the circular arrangement of the characters. Circles were regarded as mystically perfect in the Renaissance.

THE THREE GRACES

1504 - Oil on wood, 17 x 17 cm
Chantilly, Musée Condé

In ancient mythology, the Three Graces were rather hazy figures of minor importance, being linked with the Muses. But, as understood by Renaissance Neo-Platonists (who revived the highly mystical yet in some ways sensual theories of Plato, Plotinus and other Greek philosophers), they were thought to symbolise ideal beauty. They were generally called Beauty, Youth and Joy. Joy referred to pure delight, similar to that felt when listening to music; Youth to the love of colour and shape, and Beauty to the "charm and beauty of the soul which consists of the brightness of truth and virtue," in the words of Marsilio Ficino, the 15th century Neo-Platonist writer.

This small painting, along with its companion piece for *The Vision Of A Knight* (below), was Raphael's first commission for a non-religious subject. It was probably ordered by the Borghese family in Siena and

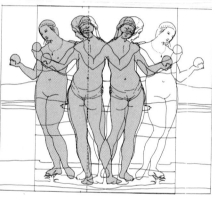

may have been intended as a confirmation gift for Scipione di Tommaso di Borghese, for it is also called *The Dream Of Scipio.* The combination of a pun on the name and a moral exhortation are typical of Renaissance love of word play. Raphael, who had not at this time started his travels around Italy, may have seen drawings of the famous classical group in Siena but he is still heavily indebted to the quattrocento art of Perugino. It has a fresh youthful charm; already Raphael is creating an ideal of female beauty. The picture is exactly the same size and shape as *The Vision Of A Knight*, showing the young hero Scipio faced with the choice between Venus and Pallas, respectively representing worldly pleasures and those of a higher nature. The two paintings probably formed a celebratory diptych (double panel) in honour of the young Scipione di Tommaso di Borghese.

The Vision of a Knight, 1504 - Oil on wood, 17 x 17 cm - London, National Gallery.
This small painting is the other part of the diptych with The Three Graces. In spite of the difference in the composition, both paintings have a similar spontaneity and structure. In one painting the structure is arranged across the picture by the prostrate figure of the knight flanked by the two figures standing on each side; in the other the equilibrium is central, contained by the three nudes.

The diagrams clearly reveal the symmetrical composition and contrapposto of the scene. The central figure with arms outstretched is seen from behind. One arm rests on the left hand figure while the other holds the apple. She appears like a mirror-image of the other two figures who are seen from the front in the same pose, holding the apples in their left and right hands. Probably in order to simplify the creation of such a contrapposto, Raphael, and later on the pupils of his studio, used a "mechanical" reflection of the outline of the central figure.

SAINT GEORGE AND THE DRAGON

1504/05 - Oil on wood, 31 x 27 cm
Paris, Musée du Louvre

Raphael painted two scenes representing Saint George slaying the dragon. Both were commissioned by Guidobaldo, Duke of Urbino. He had been made a member of the Order of the Garter and wanted to send one of them to Henry VII of England as a thankyou present, presumably recalling England's patron saint. Raphael at this stage was still receiving commissions from his native city.

In this version, the dramatic sense of movement and the prancing horse show a dynamic strength which Raphael had learnt from his studies in Florence, in particular from Leonardo's *Battle Of Anghiari*, the work begun but never finished for the Council Room in the Palazzo della Signoria. The influence of the relief of *Saint George And The Dragon* by the great 15th century sculptor Donatello is also obvious in its dramatic motion.

The scene shows Saint George in the heat of the battle. He has slackened the reins round his horse's neck and is brandishing a sword with a broad sweep of his arm. He is clearly on the point of delivering the final blow to the dragon who still has part of a spear stuck in his body. The other pieces lying shattered on the ground reveal the violence of the battle. The slender tree trunks on the left contrast with the massive figure of the now-defeated dragon.

This painting is lighter and less powerful than Raphael's other version on the same theme, harking back more clearly to his early influences. There is a Gothic element noticeable in the delicate gold edging to the saint's sword, his armour and his helmet, and the maiden's crown.

Preparatory drawing for the Paris St George And The Dragon - Pen and ink and traces of black pencil and pouncing, 26 x 27 cm - Florence, Gabinetto dei Disegni e Stampe degli Uffizi.

Paolo Uccello: St George And The Dragon, c. 1456 - Oil on canvas, 57 x 73 cm - London, National Gallery. Paolo Uccello was one of the great pioneers of both perspective and of painting in oil on canvas in the quattrocento. The English art critic Ruskin in fact attributed the perfection of perspective to Uccello, adding that "he went off his head with love of it". In this painting by Paolo Uccello, the spear held by the Saint diagonally crosses the space of the canvas to pierce the dragon's head. The perspective lines in the part of the canvas marked out by the grass diminish as they disappear erratically into the distance, finally producing two distinct horizon lines, with the object of increasing the dramatic effect and expressing movement.

In this version of Raphael's St George And The Dragon, as in the previous one, the composition is arranged in a triangle formed by the horse, the rider and the dragon. The strength of the composition is further increased by the intersection of the lines created by the pieces of broken spear on the ground.

THE LADY WITH THE UNICORN

1506/08 - Oil on wood, 65 x 51 cm
Rome, Galleria Borghese

Before this painting had been restored, it was thought to represent the martyrdom of Saint Catherine. But it turned out that the relevant symbols of her unpleasant death (details such as the mantle, the wheel and the palm) had been added later by a different hand. After X-rays revealed the original picture of the woman with the unicorn and the painting had subsequently been restored, it was finally attributed to Raphael, although the date is uncertain. Against the background of a landscape framed by two columns, the painting shows a woman with a unicorn, perennial symbol of chastity, on her lap.

The composition has clearly been heavily influenced by that of Leonardo's *Mona Lisa,* painted around this time, which Raphael admired in Florence. But that picture's heavy colours, the shadowy background and the mysterious atmosphere are totally different from the luminosity and delicate tones of this early work by Raphael, which reveals clearly the influence of Piero della Francesca. The young woman represented here may be Maddalena Doni, the wife of Agnolo Doni. He was a wealthy wool merchant who, according to Vasari "was very careful with his money in other ways but spent it readily, but still carefully, on paintings and sculptures which gave him great pleasure." He commissioned a portrait of himself and his wife, standing over their son Giovanbattista.

This portrait became justly famous for its perfect balance between form (drawing) and colour, the harmony and clearness of its tones, and the juxtaposition of the colours (the pale green of the bodice edged with dark velvet and the wide red sleeves with the white puffs). Notable too is the originality of the animal in the woman's lap - a baby unicorn which somehow resembles a lamb. The figure of the woman, with the landscape of blue hills visible through the window, is in perfect harmony with the atmosphere of the transparent sky above a low horizon which divides the painting in two halves. This is a very fine, even noble, portrait, although not as famous as *La Velata* (below: the Veiled Woman), who may be the same as the woman called La Fornarina - thought to be Raphael's mistress in his Roman years. Raphael was always sensitive to female beauty - indeed Vasari says he could not live without a mistress - and he created in his portraits an evolving ideal of female beauty which he claimed to find as much in his mind as in any real woman.

Young Woman In Front Of A Window - *Pen and ink, 22 x 16 cm - Paris, Musée du Louvre, Cabinet des Dessins. The drawing could be a sketch for this portrait by Raphael, but it is also reminiscent of a study for a studio work.*

Portrait Of A Woman (La Muta), *1507 - Oil on wood, 64 x 48 cm - Urbino, Galleria Nazionale delle Marche. This is one portrait in which the characterisation of the sitter is particularly successful.*

Portrait of a Woman (La Velata), *1516 - Oil on wood, 85 x 64 cm - Florence, Palazzo Pitti. This is one of Raphael's greatest and most famous portraits, partly because it is reputed to be that of his mistress, La Fornarina.*

THE ENTOMBMENT

1507 Oil on panel, 184 x 176 cm
Rome, Galleria Borghese

This is the most ambitious work Raphael executed before going to Rome. He was commissioned to paint an altarpiece by Atalanta Baglioni for her new chapel in Prato, in memory of her murdered son. She asked that her own suffering should be reflected in that of the Virgin. The tortuous, lengthy preparation of the altarpiece, originally intended to be a Lamentation, can be followed through at least 16 preparatory drawings before the final version. This was made by combining two cartoons which differed both in the composition and the proportions of the figures, but which shared the same triangular composition. Although obliged somehow to include the rather unorthodox episode of Christ's Mother fainting, Raphael was determined to use the motif of Christ's dangling right arm, which so starkly conveys the deadness of the corpse. This pose came both from Michelangelo's *Pietà* and from drawings by Filipino Lippi. The final painting brings together almost everything which Raphael had learned in his years in

Florence. The strength of the figures comes from the massive forms of the contemporary artist Fra Bartolemmeo, and the agitated gestures of the women derive from Donatello and Lippi.

There is not a fully unified composition (the figures seem to be pulling in opposite directions and do not fit completely into the landscape) but its brilliant, jewel-like colours and the intensity of emotions expressed do make it a work of real beauty and feeling.

This fascinating preliminary drawing expresses the painter's first idea with great immediacy and faithfulness. It also confirms his original inspiration, as well as his instinctive compositional skills and his rigorous geometrical approach to structure, which resulted in that kind of order and perfection which fixed the event in everyone's mind.

The most striking and moving aspect of this tormented painting are the faces of the characters. It would be difficult to forget the sorrowful expression of profoundly human suffering shown on the face of the Son of God; the dazed, desperate look on the face of one of the women; and the absorbed, contained expression of grief of one of the bystanders. Each character, each face, portrays the suffering caused by the tragic event they are witnessing.

THE MADONNA OF THE GOLDFINCH

1507 - Oil on wood, 107 x 77 cm
Florence, Uffizi Gallery

This, one of his last works before he left for Rome, shows Raphael more clearly under Michelangelo's influence than any of his other Madonnas of the period. Michelangelo's *Taddei Tondo* (now in the Royal Academy) had shown a muscular, active holy baby, very different from the placid infants of convention. Such athleticism was foreign to Raphael's art; here the infant Christ stretches rather languidly towards his playmate the young Saint John the Baptist, rather than recoiling strongly away from him as in Michelangelo's work. Saint John is offering a goldfinch to Christ, which was a symbol of the soul and, more specifically, of Christ's future Passion. This device was also borrowed from Michelangelo.

Raphael shows great tenderness in this painting, in the very natural poses and attitudes of the children, and especially in the relationship between the Madonna and Christ. He leans on her knee and places

His tiny foot upon hers. Typical too of this period of Raphael's art are the sweetness of the Madonna herself - another of Raphael's beautiful women - and the landscape. This now fully incorporates the advances of the High Renaissance with its realism softened by an ideal golden light.

The influence of Venetian landscape painters like Giorgione, evident here, has led to the suggestion that Raphael may have visited northern Italy around this time to see Venetian art at first hand.

The composition of the picture of the Madonna with the Child and St John is strongly influenced by Leonardo's pyramidical groupings. The figures are contained within a triangle with the Virgin Mary positioned on its axis. This triangle encloses the characters in a geometric and symbolic unity.

This detail of the goldfinch (above) gives the painting its name, symbolising the love reflected in the hands of the two children. They touch as they stroke the soft feathers of the little bird -

another detail which confirms Raphael's skill at bringing out every aspect of his characters to make them more familiar and more real, as with the Madonna's book (above) which she stops

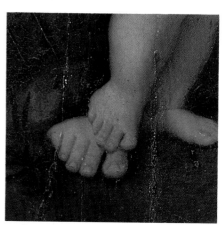

reading to look at the children, or in the way Christ's foot rests on hers (right). The whole work emphasises the humanity of the scene in spite of the divine nature of the participants.

THE DISPUTA

1509/10 - Fresco, base 770 cm Rome
Vatican Palace, Stanza della Segnatura

This is the first of the famous frescoes that Raphael painted when he was summonded to Rome by the new Pope Julius II in 1508. Julius wished to employ the greatest artists of the age to transform the city into a new, elegant capital of Christendom. Raphael, as one of a group of artists, was to paint frescoes in Julius' private apartments. In this Stanza (room) known as the Stanza della Segnatura, were the two following frescoes, *The Disputà* and *The School Of Athens*. *The Disputà* received its name from Vasari's desription (in his *Lives O f The Artists*) of the saintly men and theologians debating ("disputano") the central mysteries of the Catholic faith. Over 40 surviving drawings reveal how hard Raphael worked at the figures, redrawing their gestures and clothes frequently for this, his first really large-scale work. The lower section reveals the flowering of Raphael's genius. Never before had he painted so many almost lifesize figures in a clear, convincing manner. He has arranged individuals in small clusters, then put them in larger groups. There is no confused jumble of characters as in *The Entombment* (page 12). Instead there is a harmonious symmetry, almost musical in its balance, which centres on the altar. Above the altar, in the centre of the painting, the Dove of the Holy Spirit descends, linking the heavenly characters with the earthly ones below. The Host (the consecrated bread for the Mass) is just visible on the altar .

The strongest single influence on Raphael here is Fra Bartolommeo, whose works he had studied in Florence. The beautiful, subtle colouring of these frescoes derives from the Florentine friar, as does

The structure of this great painting is both extremely powerful and yet simple. It is centred on the Dove of the Holy Spirit, who descends from God the Father on high, past Christ to the Host, scarcely visible, on the altarpiece, itself firmly in the middle of the lower circle. Pictorial space is transformed into a symbolic and hierarchical space.

the strength of his figures, but Raphael incorporates discoveries he had made in Rome. The portraits of Fra Angelico (extreme left) and Sixtus IV (the first pope on the right) are taken from portraits on their tombs in the city. Many of the figures are clearly identifiable; Dante, the great poet, with his laurel crown, stands behind Sixtus; of the theologians six are identifi-

able by name, including Saint Jerome with his lion.

In the heavenly sphere, the apostles, starting with Saint Peter on the extreme left, and Old Testament figures like Adam and King David (on the left with his harp) echo the earthly dispute, while Saint John the Baptist and the Virgin flank Christ. Above them God the Father looks down on heaven and earth.

In the first plan for The Disputà (Chantilly, Musée Condé), which is illustrated in this bistre and white lead sketch, the composition is still far from the large scale vision of the final fresco. In particular it does not have the perspective order based on the two parallel arcs which open up the wall, producing a circular space in which the action takes place. (The young Raphael had already used this technique in The Marriage Of The Virgin on page 6).

THE SCHOOL OF ATHENS

1510/11 - Fresco, base 770 cm - Rome
Vatican Palace, Stanza della Segnatura

The *School Of Athens* faces *The Disputà*, presenting the theme of secular or pagan, as opposed to sacred Christian, learning. The liberal spirit of the age wished to demonstrate their recognition of both pagan and Christian learning, which explains this pagan presence in the papal chambers.

In a hall of great architectural grandeur and stunningly deep perspective, men from all branches of ancient knowledge write, think, debate, exhibit and explain their respective studies.

Raphael here appears to be the direct heir of great 15th century artists such as Masaccio and Piero della Francesca with their fascination with perspective. Numerous figures are arranged in a deep, mathematically constructed space. The receding arches frame the central figures of the two greatest pagan philosophers, Plato, holding his work *Timaeus,* and Aristotle with his *Ethics.* Their heads and shoulders are framed against the blue open sky. Plato points up towards heaven while Aristotle extends his hand in a finely rhetori-

In the diagram on the left, the part drawn in blue demonstrates the architectural structure which is the setting for the scene. The part drawn in black shows up the characters within the architectural composition, of which they are a vital part.

cal gesture. Plato's features may have been modelled on those of the elderly Leonardo.

Around them are groups of eager students and teachers, some of them identifiable. Socrates, another great philosopher, is arguing furiously to Plato's left, his features taken from an antique bust of him. Amongst his disciples Alcibiades, the Athenian general, can be recognised in armour. In the foreground, just to the right of the projecting door, sits the mystic and

mathematician Pythagoras, with a book and inkwell. Behind him a turbaned figure who may represent the great Muslim mathematician Averroes (one of the few moderner figures) bends attentively forward. In front, a young student holds a slate with musical notations on it. On the opposite side, Euclid demonstrates a mathematical theorem with his compasses. On the golden rim of his robe Raphael has signed the fresco by writing his own name. Behind Euclid, the Persian prophet

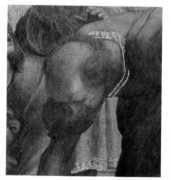

The central characters who are the focal point of the entire perspective stand out among the numerous figures: Plato and Aristotle who form the ideal focus of the entire composition. Raphael has given the historical characters in the School a resemblance to several well-known figures of his time. Thus, it may be possible to recognize Leonardo's features in Plato, Michelangelo's in what may be Heraclitus, and Bramante's in Euclid. Raphael himself can definitely be seen in the young man with the beret on the far right, next to Sodoma, his collaborator and rival.

Zoroaster holds a globe. On the extreme right, Raphael has painted his own portrait and also that of Sodoma, a colleague working with him in creating the frescoes. Sprawling inelegantly in the centre on the marble step, Diogenes, the Cynic, founder of the "negative" Cynical school of philosophy, produces the only uncouth note in a picture otherwise elegant and serenely harmonious. The older men all look nobly wise and most distinguished and their young disciples universally handsome and well-groomed. Indeed there is a danger that the characters in this fresco could appear too perfect and almost insipid. The youth in the pinkish robe on the left has an almost unrealistic sweetness of feature.

What saves Raphael's work from appearing too ideal is that the characters are set against his majestic architecture. Following the (erroneous) tradition that the philosophers of ancient Greece and Rome used to debate in the public baths, Raphael studied the immense ruins of the Baths of Caracalla and Diocletian in Rome, then far more intact than today. Clearly he has set his School in an idealised reconstruction of such a building. It echoes plans of the architect Bramante for Saint Peter's. Its huge coffered ceiling - divided into recessed segments - soars above the squabbling of the schools, suggesting a heavenly harmony that reigns over all.

The Expulsion Of Heliodorus From The Temple, 1512/13 - Fresco, base 750 cm - Rome, Vatican Palace, Stanza di Eliodoro.
This fresco, another great triumph of perspective, gave Raphael his first chance to depict violent action on a huge scale, revealing the impact of Michelangelo's recent work in the Sistine Chapel ceiling. It shows Heliodorus, a Syrian who attempted to steal the Temple treasures, being flogged by angelic guardians and simultaneously knocked down by the horse, also ridden by an angel. By the altar in the centre, a high priest is praying fervently. Pope Julius II insisted on being painted, rather incongruously, into the scene; he is being carried by bearers on the left. Vasari said that it was meant to symbolise avarice being driven out of the church; alternatively, it may refer to Julius' many wars to regain control of the Papal States in central Italy.

THE TRIUMPH OF GALATEA

c. 1512 - Fresco, 295 x 225 cm
Rome, Villa Farnesina

Agostino Chigi, the Sienese banker and the richest man in Rome, built for himself a new villa beside the Tiber. It soon became a meeting-place for cardinals, scholars, nobles and courtesans who were entertained at splendid banquets. (At one of these, Chigi invited his guests to throw all the gold and silver plates off which they had eaten into the river; unknown to them, he had nets hung in the water to catch the plates as they fell). Chigi was also a perceptive patron of the arts and he commissioned Raphael to decorate part of his new villa with frescoes.

In a letter to Castiglione, Raphael wrote that to portray a beautiful woman "I use a certain idea which comes into my mind." Raphael's ideas of perfect beauty, derived from Plato, shaped the features of almost every woman he painted; *Galatea* portrays not a specific woman, but an ideal of beauty.

Galatea was a beautiful sea nymph with whom the cyclops Polyphemus fell in love. Raphael shows her being carried over the waves in a dolphin-drawn shell surrounded by Tritons and Nereids all engaged in gently erotic dalliance.

This was meant to be one of a series of frescoes, but only Galatea was finished, perhaps because floods damaged the villa in 1514. The amount of a day's work can be seen in the change in the shade of blue marked by the bow of the cupid on the right. Raphael tried to avoid matching each successive day's blue (which dried at differing rates depending on the weather) by choosing some such marker. Despite its wonderful freshness, this picture reveals archaeological sources. Raphael had clearly never seen a real dolphin, hence these odd fish; the horse is marmoreal in colour and pose, showing it was copied from an antique statue.

In the diagram which shows the arrangement of the characters, Galatea is at the centre on the vertical axis, contained in a triangle, but she is also at the centre of a circle whose diameter equals half the height of the painting. The three cupids are placed in a semi-circle above, while the shell and the cherub are in another below.

St Catherine of Alexandria, 1508 - Oil on wood, 71 x 53 cm - London, National Gallery. Apart from the spiked wheel, the traditional iconographic attributes of crown, sword and book, are absent. Though modified in essence, the pose of the female figure recalls the pose of the goddess Galatea on a shell, pulled by dolphins.

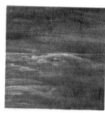
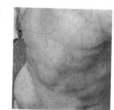

Raphael's choice of colours produces the crystalline light illuminating the scene; in particular the green marbled tones of the surface of the sea; the white and blue of the sky dotted with clouds; the dense red of Galatea's cloak which stands out against the background, while also framing the gold of her hair; and the pink and brown tones of the naked bodies of the sea gods.

THE LIBERATION OF SAINT PETER

1513/14 - Fresco, base 660 cm
Rome, Vatican Palace, Stanza di Eliodoro

This was the last fresco painted by Raphael for Pope Julius II. The story is of Saint Peter being freed by an angel from his imprisionment by King Herod. It was of special interest to Julius not only because it showed divine intervention on behalf of the very first pope, Saint Peter but also as it had a direct reference to Julius' title as Cardinal of San Pietro in Vinicoli (Saint Peter in chains). It has even been suggested that Raphael painted Saint Peter with the pope's features, though this is debatable.

This is one of the earliest night scenes in Italian art. Light is extremely important in the whole picture, as can be seen from its reproduction in entirety below. The radiant angel is very original; it was described by a contemporary as being "composed of air and light, without mortal weight". The painting has been compared favourably since then to Rembrandt's *Nightwatch*. The prison itself is also

The diagram of the central part of the fresco reveals a triangle which contains the figure of the saint and that of the angel. This triangle has been superimposed on another, inverted triangle, which determines the way the soldiers are leaning against the wall.

graphically and originally horrible. Raphael appears to have been influenced by atmospheric Venetian paintings in the exterior scene on the left, with clouds scudding across the moon and the dramatic actions of the guards, with their figures highlighted by the reflections of the torches on their armour.

The fresco develops as a real story, with the release of the saint in the centre, the stupefied amazement of the guards who have just woken up on the left, and on the right the angel who has freed Peter leading him out past the figures of the soldiers who are still sleeping.

POPE LEO X AND CARDINALS
GIULIO DE MEDICI AND LUIGI ROSSI

1518/19 - Oil on wood, 154 x 119 cm
Florence, Uffizi Gallery

This is a splendid portrait, both majestically imposing and psychologically revealing.

Leo X had become pope in 1513, in succession, and total contrast, to Julius II. Unlike the warlike Julius, Leo X, a Medici, was peaceful, amiable and pleasure-loving. On being elected, he is reputed to have said: "Now God has given us the papacy, let us enjoy it". But he was also, and fittingly for a Medici, extremely cultured. Under him, the High Renaissance in Rome entered its last and most glorious phase.

Leo's cousin Giulio had been made archbishop of Florence to strengthen Medici control of that city (to which they had returned in 1512) and Rossi had been made a cardinal in 1517. It could therefore be considered a political statement, to be expected at the court of a great Renaissance prince - which is how Leo behaved.

Vasari admired this portrait especially, dwelling on its sumptuousness: "the velvet with its pile, the damask which the Pope wears, rustling and shiny, the fur linings soft and lively and the golds and silks so well imitated that they seem not paint but actual gold and silk. Among other things there is the ball on the chair, burnished with gold, which reflects, like a mirror, the lights of the windows..." The ball is in fact a piece of family heraldry, referring to the Medici insignia, the palla (ball).

The concept of a triple portrait was entirely new; the two cardinals push forward to emphasize the central figure of the plump, short-sighted Pope, who sits holding a magnifying glass to study the bible.

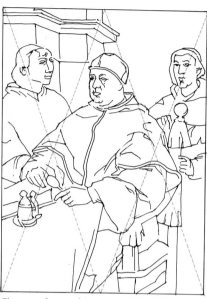

The main figure of the scene, that of Pope Leo X, is contained within a triangle which has been superimposed, inverted, on the triangle which defines the characters on each side of the pope.

Portrait Of Baldassare Castiglione, 1514-1515 - Oil on canvas, 86 x 67 cm - Paris, Louvre. Painted by Raphael a few years before the portrait of Leo X, this is one of the greatest portraits of the Renaissance. Baldassare Castiglione was the author of the famous book The Courtier which he set in Raphael's native Urbino. He is shown looking superbly dignified yet very human, his blue eyes especially noticeable. Castiglione was in fact quite bald - one reason he is wearing such a fine hat.

Raphael devoted great care and attention to every detail. The book which the Pope is reading is clearly identifiable as the Hamilton Bible while the bell is brilliantly depicted.

THE TRANSFIGURATION

1518-1520 - Oil on wood, 405 x 278 cm
Rome, Vatican Library.

This stunning and ambitiously large painting was commissioned from Raphael by Cardinal Giulio Medici for the cathedral of Narbonne of which he was the archbishop, although it was never delivered. The restoration of this painting in 1981 revealed the brilliance of its colours and confirmed that the entire project was the work of Raphael. Until then, it had been thought that the lower section of the painting had only been sketched out when the artist died and that it was subsequently completed by his pupil Giulio Romano.

The drama and movement of this painting show Raphael looking back to Leonardo, to his study for *The Battle Of Anghiari* and to his unfinished *Adoration,* both in Florence. Raphael here adopted Leonardo's dark shadows, using printer's lampblack for them - an innovation Vasari thought very rash. Raphael shows Jesus ascending to heaven, flanked by Moses and Elijah, and watched by Peter, James and John. In the lower section, the apostles and the crowd are gesticulating wildly with their arms and hands. This is particularly effective as the apostles are lit only from behind, unlike the crowd in the foreground. The whole composition is complex and articulate, characterized by strong contrasts of light and shadow.

The scene above is bright and shining, orderly and symmetrical, surging up to heaven. Below, all is tumult in the excited clash of light and shade, the interweaving of limbs and arms with hands pointing. All this melodrama is far from the serene classicism which Raphael had made his hallmark in the previous 13 years in Rome. In fact it anticipates some of the aspects of Mannerism, which his pupils like Giulio Romano developed out of the High Renaissance after his death, particularly in its rather harsh, acid colours and in its elongated treatment of the female form, noticeable in the woman in the foreground. Raphael on his death bed reputedly had this monumental work placed in front of him, so that he could look at it in his last moments. Raphael, torn from life at the height of his powers, wanted to close his eyes on a vision of heavenly glory.

In the final composition the scene is divided into two separate zones, the lower one (two thirds the height of the painting) devoted to earthly characters who are excited and a higher part (one third of the height) devoted to the characters soaring into heaven. The axes dividing the picture into these spaces join the circle which holds and contains the dominant figures.

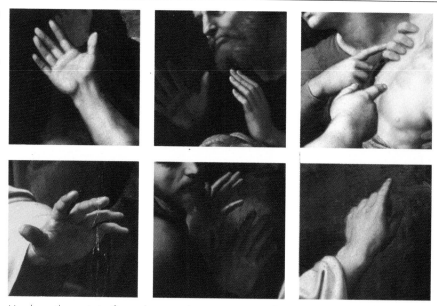

Hands are the most significant element in their various attitudes. This is particularly so in the sequence which, seem to express the journey of man to salvation, the truth and life (with the finger of the apostle on the left pointing to Christ ascending to heaven).

A PERFECT PAINTER ?

Few painters or artists have suffered so much from over-enthusiastic admirers as Raphael; few have had so many myths woven around them. Adjectives such as "divine" and "sublime" have been liberally used to describe Raphael himself and his style. These terms have obscured our understanding of the works of one of the greatest of all artists. This is particularly the case for the general public, who cannot find in Raphael's story any signs of the human suffering, romantic melodramas or other colourful eccentricities which are sometimes thought to be the inevitable accompaniment of real genius. Raphael was not unrecognised or unpraised in his own lifetime; he did not go mad, nor suffer persecution or poverty, nor did he experience the full horrors of war; his health seems to have been excellent up to his early death; far from going around in rags, grunting at people and locking himself away for weeks at a stretch like Michelangelo, he was well-dressed, well-behaved and very sociable.

Except for his reputedly over-strenuous lovelife, Raphael's life - and his work, with its relentless idealism - may strike the modern observer as insipid and blan to the point of being boring.

With Raphael everythin seems calm, harmonious, symme rical, perfectly arranged and u troubled. Nothing ignoble, undi nified or indecent could real upset these beautiful madonna noble philosophers or handsom youths. For all their apparent rea ism, they exist more in the world ideal, immortal forms of Plato philosophy, then so very influe tial, than they do in reality. In th sense, his works can be defined standing at the peak of the art the Renaissance, with its idealisin

RAPHAEL AND HIS TIMES

	HIS LIFE AND WORKS	HISTORY	ART AND CULTURE
1483	Raffaello Sanzio, called Raphael, born on Good Friday at Urbino in central Italy	Death of Louis XI of France; Charles VIII succeeds him Death of Edward IV in England; Richard of York usurps the throne and imprisons the princes in the Tower, probably murdering them Birth of Martin Luther	Leonardo da Vinci starts *The Virgin On The Rocks* First version of German legend *Till Eulenspiegel*
1494	Orphaned at the age of 11. Starts working in Perugino's studio	Charles VIII invades Italy, starting the Italian Wars Florence expels the Medici family and becomes a Republic under the influence of the Dominican friar Savanorola Sir Robert Clifford reveals a plot to murder Henry VII	Jean Bourdichon: *Madonna And Child With Saints*
1498	By now producing works indistinguishable from those of his master Perugino	Louis XII becomes king of France; renews the Italian wars with an attack on Milan Savanorola hanged and his body burnt Vasco da Gama discovers sea route to India	Master of Moulins: *The Moulins Triptych* John Skelton: *The Bowge Of Court*
1504	Leaves for Florence where he remains until 1508, though making journeys elsewhere. Paints *The Marriage Of The Virgin*	Statute Against Retaining bans private militias in England Cesare Borgia loses his conquests in central Italy	Michelangelo finishes his *David* Lucas Cranach: *Rest On The Flight Into Egypt* Henry VII chapel built at Westminster Abbey
1505	Finishes *Saint George And The Dragon*, starts *The Lady With The Unicorn*	The Portugese arrive in Ceylon The Spanish seize Mers-el-Kebir	Michelangelo summoned to Rome by Julius II Leonardo working on *The Mona Lisa* Albrecht Dürer visits Venice
1507	Paints *The Entombment* and *The Madonna Of The Goldfinch*	Unity of the Holy Roman Empire (of Germany) recognised at the Diet of Constance	Giorgione: *The Dresden Venus: The Three Philosophers* Titian working with Giorgione on the frescoes for the Fondaco dei Tedeschi

endencies, its reverence for classical antiquity and its passionate love of a beauty thought to be both physical and spiritual.

What this view ignores is the fact that this ideal "peak" was created at the centre of often violent political events (the bloody Italian wars raged throughout his life, with the peninsula becoming the battlefield for half Europe) and in only a few years. Also, that its creator was a young man who had to compete - and at times to co-exist - with the two established giants, Leonardo and Michelangelo. The glory of Raphael is that he found a "third way", which combined with and finally surpassed most of the other art of his time (including even some influences from distant Venice). During the 20 or so years of the High Renaissance (1500-1520) Raphael first learnt from the two older artists and then in some ways overtook them. He established and defined the canons of classical art so clearly that his art would seem a tyranny to some later painters.

It is not by chance that Raphael was born in Urbino on the fringes of the most courtly society in Europe. Federigo da Montefeltro had built the ducal palace and started the ducal collection, with Piero della Francesca, the great quattrocento (15th century) master, working for him; his successor Guidobaldo, after a short exile, in 1504 established the court which Baldassare Castiglione has immortalised in his book *The Courtier*.

This book gave the concept of the gentleman probably its noblest definition as someone cultured, well-mannered, gracious and courteous in all his dealings - very like Raphael in real life.

There were no artists working in Urbino of the stature of Piero

1508	Leaves for Rome, where Bramante, also from Urbino, introduces him to papal court. Paints *The Esterhazy Madonna*	League of Cambrai unites all Europe against Venice Portugese under Albuquerque capture Socotra	Bramante starts building the new Saint Peter's in Rome Birth of Palladio
1509	Working on the frescoes for the Stanza della Segnatura in the Vatican, soon becoming Julius II's favourite painter	Henry VIII becomes king of England on the death of Henry VII League of Cambrai defeats Venice at Battle of Agnello Birth of John Calvin	Work restarted on King's College Chapel, Cambridge Durer finishes the reredos for the Heller family Lucas Cranach: *The Torgau Reredos*
1511	Finishes the Stanza della Segnatura frescoes, starts work on the Stanza di Eliodoro	Julius II forms a "Holy League" of European powers to drive the French out of Italy	Luther becomes professor at Wittenberg University Erasmus: *The Praise Of Folly*
1513	The new pope, Leo X, also treats Raphael as his favourite painter. Starts work on *The Liberation Of Saint Peter*	Death of Julius II; Leo X becomes pope France is beaten at Battle of Novara by Holy League English defeat French at the Battle of the Spurs and the Scots at the Battle of Flodden	Machiavelli: *The Prince* Matthys Grünewald: *The Issenheim Reredos*
1514	Becomes architect of Saint Peter's on the death of Bramante. Starts work on the Stanza dell'Incendio frescoes	Lorenzo de Medici becomes ruler of Florence Peace between England and France, which cedes Tournai	Andrea del Sarto: *Birth Of The Virgin* John Skelton: *Ballad Of The Scottish King*
1515	Starts work on the series of cartoons for the tapestries of *The Acts Of The Apostles*	Francis I becomes King of France aand invades Italy; defeats the Swiss at the Battle of Marignano	King's College Chapel completed Hans Holbein: *Danse Macabre*
1519	Completes his *Portrait Of Leo X With Cardinals Giulio de Medici and Luigi Rossi*. Works on decorating the Vatican Loggia	Charles V becomes Emperor of Germany, King of Spain and Duke of Burgundy, so upsetting the balance of power in Europe	Michelangelo starts work on the Medici tombs in Florence Death of Leonardo da Vinci and John Colet
1520	Dies suddenly April 6, probably of a malarial fever	Success of the Reformation in Germany; Luther burns papal bull of excommunication in Wittenberg Field of the Cloth of Gold; ceremonial meeting between Francis I and Henry VIII	Titian: *Man With A Glove* Henry VIII: *A Defence Of The Seven Sacraments*

under Guidobaldo, but Raphael would have seen and known his works with their clear expression of space, subtle colours and ordered, architectural features. These strict, austere qualities would have balanced the unvarying sweetness Raphael learnt from Perugino, explaining the power and clarity already evident in *The Marriage Of The Virgin* (page 4).

Appropriately, *The Marriage* is hung in the same room of the Brera Gallery as Piero della Francesca's Montefeltro altarpiece. This demonstrates that Raphael was the true heir of Piero, who constructed paintings within a framework of perfect geometry. The temple is drawn in perspective, and through it opens the door giving onto the blue void of heaven. The style of the temple itself derives from the architecture of the great Bramante. Both the architect and the painter would be lifelong influences on Raphael.

When he arrived in Florence, Raphael found himself in the midst of a city acutely aware of its previous wonderful century of artistic discovery and determined to carry it onward. Florence was also self-consciously republican at the time, having expelled the Medici in 1494 and declared a republic. This was, however, a republic much threatened by wars, as Spain, France, the Empire and the Papacy fought out their conflicts up and down the peninsula; it was to encourage a sense of martial patriotism among the markedly unwarlike Florentines that the competitive scheme to have Leonardo decorate one wall of the Palazzo della Signoria (town hall) and Michelangelo the other with battle scenes was conceived. The scheme was a failure, neither of the two greatest living painters finishing their works (which have since been destroyed); the Republic itself did not last very long, but in his four years there Raphael was able to observe and absorb all that they could teach him.

A painting which exemplifies this absorption of what he learned from others is *The Entombment* (page 12) executed in 1507 for Atalanta Baglioni of Perugia. The examples of Michelangelo are consciously quoted in the interlocking, heroic bodies, while there is a suggestion of classical sculpture, in particular of an antique relief depicting the funeral rites of Meleager.

THE RENAISSANCE'S ZENITH

When Pope Julius II's commission to decorate the Vatican apartments - the Stanze - called Raphael to Rome, he took with him invaluable lessons. His days of study were now over; the days of achievement were about to begin.

Rome, in the quattrocento only a secondary centre of the Renaissance, was under the rule of forceful popes like Alexander VII and Julius II at the very moment when the ideas and artistic developments of the earlier Renaissance came together to form the short period of the High Renaissance, from 1500 to 1520. That last date is also, significantly, the year of Raphael's death; with his death, the noon of the Renaissance was past and the Mannerist period - affected, unnaturalistic, or over-stylish - began. But its influence lasted nearly four centuries.

The classicism of the High Renaissance at first glance seems undramatic and uninteresting. *The Madonna Of The Goldfinch* (page 14) seems so simply painted that it looks easy. But tremendous planning and care went into its noble simplicity. The way the Virgin's face is moulded and recedes into the shade, the way Raphael makes us feel the volume of her body loosely wrapped in her mantle, show an art which has arrived at that fusion of serene idealism and physical realism for which the earlier Renaissance had long striven.

The same fusion of the ideal and the actual is evident in his great frescoes for the Stanze della Segnatura (pages 16-21). Their iconographic themes may not have been chosen by the 28-year-old painter, as Michelangelo chose his for the Sistine Chapel, yet the handling of them is Raphael's own. The philosophers in *The School of Athens* rival Michelangelo's figures in heroic stature but their mood is one of a golden serenity the Tuscan never reached. If wisdom can be attained through philosophical discussions, we can feel certain that Raphael's sages will do so.

The perfect balance of the picture - so subtle that it may go unnoticed - is also found in a completely different work, *The Triumph Of Galatea* (page 22). The sea-nymph rides across the waves in her dolphin-drawn chariot, other sea-gods and nymphs milling around her. Every figure in this joyful picture is balanced harmoniously, from the cupids aiming arrows down on the crowd to sea-gods wheeling around the nymph.

When he had finished his *Galatea*, Raphael was asked where on earth he had found the model for such happy beauty. He replied that he had not copied any specific model but had followed "a certain idea in his mind". This ideal of female beauty is repeated in many of Raphael's later Madonnas and portraits, including the famous *La Velata* (veiled lady) whom Vasari thought was his mistress. But Raphael never lost touch with reality, as is clear from his superb portrait of *Leo X,* for example (page 26).

Like Mozart, who died at much the same age, Raphael brought the classical tradition to perfection and died just before it, and the world which had fostered it, fell apart. Within seven years of his death Rome was sacked by mutinying German troops, its courtiers dispersed, its harmony shattered - except in the works of Raphael, which remained, resplendent and serene, to entrance future generations of artists with visions of perfection.